EIGHTEENTH-CENTURY LITERATURE AND CULTURE

INTRODUCTIONS TO BRITISH LITERATURE AND CULTURE SERIES

Medieval Literature and Culture by Andrew Galloway
Renaissance Literature and Culture by Matthew Steggle and Lisa Hopkins
Seventeenth-Century Literature and Culture by Jim Daems
Victorian Literature and Culture by Maureen Moran
Romanticism by Sharon Ruston
Modernism by Leigh Wilson

EIGHTEENTH-CENTURY LITERATURE AND CULTURE

Paul Goring

continuum

Continuum

The Tower Building
11 York Road
London SE1 7NX
www.continuumbooks.com

80 Maiden Lane
Suite 704
New York, NY 10038

First published 2008

British Library Cataloguing-in-Publication Data
A catalogue record for this book is available from the British Library.

ISBN: 978-0-8264-8564-9
      978-0-8264-8565-6

Library of Congress Cataloging-in-Publication Data
A catalog record for this book is available from the Library of Congress.

Typeset by Servis Filmsetting Ltd, Manchester
Printed and bound in Great Britain by MPG Books Ltd, Bodmin, Cornwall.

Contents

Acknowledgements

I began writing this book in the final weeks of a fellowship at the University of St Andrews. I am grateful to the family of J. D. Fleeman who set up the fellowship and to the staff in the Department of English who helped make my stay such an enjoyable one – particular thanks to Nick Roe, Tom Jones and Katie Halsey who generously shared useful ideas and suggestions. Many other friends and scholars have provided assistance of various kinds as the book has progressed, and I must mention particularly Jeremy Hawthorn, Domhnall Mitchell, Shaun Regan, Eli Løfaldli, and Juan Pellicer whose comments on draft sections have been invaluable. For arranging matters so that I could have an extended visit to the British Library in London to finish the book, I am very grateful to Arne Halvorsen and Dagny Causse.

Given the book's nature, I would like to take this opportunity to thank the many scholars who in their various capacities as teachers, colleagues and friends have inspired and fuelled my interest in eighteenth-century Britain and its authors – particular thanks to Peter Miles, Rebecca Ferguson, Ian Bell, David Shuttleton, Brean Hammond, Thomas Keymer, Peter de Voogd and Matthew Grenby. Thanks too to my students who, over the years, have forced me to reconsider matters addressed in the book and have unknowingly helped me to formulate and present this discussion.

Finally, sincere thanks are due to the fine team at Continuum – particularly Anna Sandeman for her enthusiasm and patience – and to my friends and family, especially Tone Midtgård, for encouragement and for putting up with my being self-absorbed to a quite unseemly degree during phases of writing.

For readers able to pronounce Norwegian,
this book is dedicated to
Tone

For those who can't, it is dedicated to
Victoria

Introduction

This book aims to give a broad introduction to British literature and to the circumstances in which literature was written
and read between the years 1688 and 1789. It is not an introduction to specific literary works from that period, but is
rather an account of the society which stimulated and supported a rich culture of literary production and of the major
currents within that culture. What type of society were writers
and readers of the time inhabiting? What place did writing
and reading have in that society? What systems of thought and
belief were subscribed to at the time? What were the major
genres? The aim is to address questions such as these so as to
begin to build up a context for reading eighteenth-century
British literature with an informed sense of the circumstances
of its original production and consumption.

The years chosen as start and end points for this account
were each marked by revolutions which had major, life-
changing repercussions for both Britain and the wider world.
The first – the so-called 'Glorious Revolution' of 1688–89 –
was centred within Britain and had hugely significant consequences for British political, social and religious life in the
years which followed. The French Revolution of 1789 was
external to Britain, but it nonetheless provoked major shifts
within British political discourse, such that 1789 can be seen
as a watershed year within the history of Britain. These are,
of course, not the only years which could have been chosen
– the parameters of historical periods are always somewhat
arbitrary, and doubtless there are historians and literary

historians who would prefer alternative years. Many scholars, for example, find it useful to demarcate a 'long eighteenth century' from the restoration of the monarchy in 1660 to the Reform Act of 1832. Nonetheless, 1688 and 1789 serve as well as most historical bookends, and, particularly in the case of the earlier year, there is a firmer grounding in 'event' than with the more convenient 1700 and 1800, the choice of which could have added precision to a discussion of 'the eighteenth century' and 'eighteenth-century literature'. For ease in what follows, I shall use those phrases even though the period under scrutiny does not map precisely onto the official century.

Many aspects of British life during this period were extremely different from the conditions we now find in Britain at the beginning of the twenty-first century. For one thing, at least at the start of the period, 'Britain' itself had not yet come into being – this composite nation, in fact, was one of the innovations of the eighteenth century. England and Wales had long been officially united, but until 1707 Scotland was still politically independent, despite being joined to its southern neighbours through a monarchical union. Throughout the period, Ireland had the status of a colony – it would not become an official part of Britain until the Act of Union of 1800. These territories were peopled comparatively sparsely – the total population of England, Wales, Scotland and Ireland rose from around 9 million in 1688 to around 14.5 million in 1789 – and most lived in rural communities. Towns and cities were growing significantly in number and size – London's population doubled to around a million during the century – and the infrastructure for transport and communication between urban centres was developing. But still a great proportion of the population worked on the land, and much of Britain's commerce was steered by the rural economy – this was a time when the quality of the annual harvest still had significance for the welfare and wealth of the nation. The people of Britain were divided according to a rigid social hierarchy in which divisions between the different social ranks were keenly felt, and such a hierarchy was widely assumed to be the natural way of the world. The aristocracy was very influential within both national and local politics, and at the top of the social order was a monarch who still had significant influence. Matters of ascendancy had great constitutional and political importance. This was also a time when most individuals believed in God and when issues of faith and religion were central to social and cultural discourse.

However, while some aspects of eighteenth-century British society may now seem alien, we also witness in the period major changes and upheavals out of which emerged many of the institutions and social practices which mark Britain today – it was a society undergoing profound transformation. British industry was growing and becoming more sophisticated – it was on the basis of eighteenth-century innovations that the accelerated industrial growth of the nineteenth century was able to occur. The foundations of modern public and private finance were being laid, with the Bank of England being established in 1694, and this enabled long-term investments which supported commercial growth. Parliament became a genuinely powerful institution which provided a permanent check against the power of the monarch. Britain was also becoming a deeply consumerist society. For those who had sufficient wealth, there was a burgeoning market offering an increasing variety of consumer goods from increasingly distant and diverse parts of the globe. This was in large part due to another key development of the period: the growth of Britain's colonial empire and the increasing significance of Britain in international affairs.

The eighteenth century, then, was a time of major changes for Britain – and they were changes in which the printed word played an important role. For one thing, printed matter as a *widely available* commodity was a further innovation of the period. The eighteenth century saw a massive expansion of the print trade; it was the first time in British history that the technology of print was harnessed for the purposes of regular, mass communication. And, as such, the printed word became a prime channel for the mediation of, reflection upon, and intervention into the many changes and upheavals which Britain was undergoing. In this respect newspapers and periodicals, of which there was a huge proliferation, were extremely important; but so too was much of the imaginative literature which is still read and studied today. Reading eighteenth-century novels, poetry and plays we again and again encounter direct or indirect commentary upon the contemporary world and the ways in which it was changing. Telling stories served the purposes of entertainment, but stories were often also a way of coming to terms with aspects of contemporary life, or a tool by which writers attempted to make a difference to the society around them. For example, Jonathan Swift's *Gulliver's Travels* (1726) – one of the classic works to come out of the period – offers a fantastic tale of travels in an unreal world, but it is *at the same time* a commentary on eighteenth-century politics, manners, science and other aspects of British society.

It is largely because so many literary works of the time were in some way negotiating contemporary issues and events that examining the circumstances in which they were produced can enrich our reading of those works now. In this short book I can provide only a sketch of eighteenth-century Britain and of the major genres and literary movements it spawned. My hope is that this will provide a useful general orientation for readers at an early stage of their encounter with eighteenth-century literature and culture, whilst also signposting some of the routes which might be followed as part of further and deeper explorations of this dynamic and exciting period of literary production.

1

Historical, Cultural and Intellectual Context

Politics and Society
Religion, Science and Philosophy
Arts and Culture

POLITICS AND SOCIETY

'The Glorious Revolution' and its consequences

Why was the revolution of 1688–89 so significant to the future development of Britain? In order to address that question, let us briefly go over what this revolution – one prompted by fierce conflicts concerning questions of religion and of who should hold the reins of power – actually entailed.

The central event of the revolution was the deposition by Parliament of James II, the Stuart monarch of England and Wales, who also ruled over Scotland as James VII. Parliament replaced James with his own daughter, Mary, and his Dutch son-in-law, William of Orange, who took the title William III. James, a Catholic, had taken the throne in 1685 on the death of his brother Charles II, and he immediately set about using his position to overturn much of the legislation which maintained the exclusion of Catholics from many areas of public life. He challenged the authority of the Church of England by seeking to establish religious equality for Catholics, he endeavoured to Catholicize his government, and he increased the size of his army and appointed a number of Catholics to officer rank. James appeared to many to be flaunting and abusing his power, and his actions provoked widespread hostility in a nation in which there was a strong strain of anti-Catholicism as well as a keen desire to protect the privileged position of the established Protestant Church.

Matters came to a head in 1688 when the birth of a son to James's Catholic wife gave rise to the prospect of a long-term Catholic monarchy – prior to the son's birth James's primary heirs were his Protestant daughters, Mary and Anne, by his first wife. A group of eminent, disaffected Protestant politicians wrote to William of Orange inviting him to invade and take the throne. William, an ardent Protestant and aggressive opponent of Louis XIV of France, had apparently already planned to do something along those lines without the invitation so as to avert a possible Catholic alliance between France and England. In November 1688 he sailed to England, landed in Devon, and advanced upon London. James's support soon collapsed and he fled to France, leaving William free to take the throne.

Early in 1689 a convention of Parliament formally invited William and Mary to rule jointly; James's flight to France was declared to be an abdication, which lent a gloss of regularity to what were, in fact, highly revolutionary events. Importantly, the invitation was accompanied by a Bill of Rights – legislation which was designed to control both the faith of the monarch as well as the reach of his or her power. This Bill declared that the succession should pass to Mary's sister, Anne, and it made it illegal for Catholics to hold the throne. In addition, it prevented the monarch from maintaining an army during peacetime, and it took from the monarch the power to abolish laws. The Bill, in other words, legislated against all that had been found offensive and threatening in James's handling of power, whilst in its very nature it asserted that the monarch should be answerable to Parliament. No longer could the monarch assert an unassailable 'divine right' to rule.

The revolution is sometimes known as the 'Bloodless Revolution', due to William's almost unopposed conquering of England and Wales, but the name becomes inappropriate when we consider what happened subsequently in Scotland and Ireland. In Scotland, James's hold on power was untenable, and later in 1689 the Scottish crown was handed to William and Mary. For many in the strongly Presbyterian Scottish Lowlands this was more palatable than the idea of a Catholic monarch, despite the affront to hereditary royal rights. Also appealing to the Presbyterians was a decree which, like the Bill of Rights in England, debarred Catholics from the Scottish throne. Remaining Scottish support for James was overcome – but not entirely eliminated – through battle, including particularly brutal attacks upon resistant clans in the Highlands where Catholicism was strong.

In Ireland, with the majority of the population Catholic, James retained widespread support, which was bolstered by forces from France – in fact, the French would long serve as backers of the Stuart cause. William set about suppressing Irish opposition through a military campaign, claiming his most significant victory at the bloody Battle of the Boyne in 1690. Thereafter the Protestant Anglican ascendancy maintained a tight control of Ireland and imposed severe strictures upon Irish Catholics, which prevented them from holding most public offices and which restricted their rights to gain or bequeath land. At the start of the eighteenth century, approximately 80 per cent of Irish land was owned by English settlers, who comprised only around 20 per cent of the population. William's consolidation of his position, then, resulted in England becoming more clearly positioned as the leading power of the British territories. The balance of power between Scotland and England shifted towards the south, while English rule over Ireland became stricter and more aggressively enforced.

To sum up, then, the most significant domestic consequences of the Glorious Revolution were these:

- Parliament became established as the primary organ of government, with which the monarch needed to collaborate
- Protestantism became more firmly secured as the established religion

- England's position as the leading power within Britain became strengthened.

Through William, Britain's position within Europe was also altered, as the country was drawn into a series of costly wars, beginning with the Nine Years' War (1689–97), which were fought primarily against France so as to restrict French international trade and colonial expansion. Prior to the revolution, Britain's foreign policy had been directed largely against the Dutch in order to protect Britain's expanding overseas trading interests. William's anti-French policy launched what would become an enduring rivalry, and despite much ongoing cultural exchange between the British and the French peoples, Britain would be at war with France on and off throughout the eighteenth century, making huge colonial gains in the process.

The revolution and the changes it brought won widespread support within Britain, but opposition to William and his successors and a desire to restore the line of James II remained alive, finding its main focus in the movement known as Jacobitism (after 'Jacobus', the Latin for James). The threat posed by the Jacobites was very considerable: many attempts to topple the monarchy were planned, and there were two major Jacobite uprisings in 1715 and 1745. The latter rebellion, led by Charles Edward Stuart (1720–88) – the 'Young Pretender' better known as 'Bonnie Prince Charlie' – was quashed at the Battle of Culloden in 1746, following which many Jacobites were killed or banished in a brutal punitive aftermath. Thereafter the movement lacked sufficient force to be a genuine danger to the establishment, but Jacobitism remained on the political map for some years more, and many remained wistfully attached to the cause even while recognizing its hopelessness. In fact, for the half century following William's takeover, Jacobitism was probably responsible for increasing support for the order it opposed, as adherents to the Protestant monarchy from across the diverse regions of Britain became united in a desire to protect the nation against further revolution.

The eighteenth century has often been seen as a comfortable

period of peace and stability for Britain, and it is true that the new constitution of 1689 put in place a system of rule which would endure without truly radical revision until the Reform Act of 1832. However, that constitution also contained the seeds of political tension and turbulence both at home and abroad, and people at the time by no means assumed that the new order would survive.

The growth of print

The social and political transformations which the revolution set in motion need to be considered further, but since our main aim here is to explore the place of literature in the eighteenth century, it will be useful at this point to look at the position which printed matter came to occupy during the period. In fact, the printing industry was another aspect of society which underwent significant change, and, as a powerful tool of communication, print was a major player in Britain's broader developments. Over the course of the period, Britain saw

- an increase in the production of reading matter
- a diversification of the types of reading matter produced
- a growth in the number of printing houses, booksellers/ publishers, and professional writers
- a development of a trade and communication network via which reading matter was distributed across the country and to individual consumers
- a large increase in the number of readers.

The printing industry, in short, became more commercialized and efficient, and in the process the printed word gained a new level of pervasiveness and importance in Britain. Why did this occur?

In the late seventeenth century, the British press was a relatively small and tightly controlled industry constrained by government regulations. The political power of print had become clear during the Civil War and Interregnum, the turmoil of which times was nourished through a proliferation of printed pamphlets. Following the restoration of the monarchy in 1660, strict controls were imposed upon the presses. The Licensing Act of 1662 limited the number of licensed printing houses, it subjected new works to pre-publication censorship, and it required them to be registered by the Stationers' Company – a type of government-sanctioned guild. As a result, the printing industry was concentrated almost exclusively in London, although there were presses in Oxford and Cambridge attached to the universities. The printing of newspapers was controlled by a government-approved monopoly – at that time, in fact, oral communication was as important as print for the dissemination of news.

In 1695, the Licensing Act was allowed to lapse – the reasons for this remain somewhat obscure, but there had been criticism of the manner in which the Act was being administered, and by this time the position of the government and of William III was more secure than just after the revolution and so fears of a freer press among the country's rulers were lessened. The Stationers' Company retained a monopoly allowing it to produce some works, but the lapsing of the Act nonetheless opened up a largely free literary marketplace and presented great new opportunities for entrepreneurial printers, booksellers, and authors. After 1695, there was no pre-publication censorship – if the government wished to suppress a published work, it had to prosecute for libel. 'The Age of Authors', as Samuel Johnson (1709–84) described his era in a 1753 essay, had dawned (Johnson 1963, 457).

Initially there was considerable opposition to a free press – not least from those printers who had lost monopolies and from churchmen who feared the circulation of non-Anglican literature. But such opposition was soon overwhelmed as upstart printers, writers and readers embraced the new opportunities presented by a free press. The printing industry grew rapidly in London. By 1720, around 70 printing firms were operating there, and the capital would remain the main centre of literary production throughout the period and beyond. Importantly, though, provincial printing houses also began to be established, largely for the production of pamphlets and local newspapers – the first was a Bristol paper launched at the beginning of the new century. By the 1750s most sizeable towns had a press and more than 30 provincial newspapers were being produced, and by the end of the century there were over 100 papers. Not all newspapers were successful – it was very much an age of experimentation in the industry, and many new publications foundered. However, a countrywide network of regular newspapers did develop and it revolutionized the dispersal of information of many kinds – not only news and opinion, but also announcements and a flood of advertisements. Indeed, in many papers news articles were heavily outweighed by advertisements.

When it came to book production, provincial printers typically played second fiddle to the industry in London. The first volumes of *Tristram Shandy* (1759–67), a serially published fiction by Laurence Sterne (1713–68), were printed in York, but it was only when Sterne broke into the London literary scene that he found real success. Nonetheless, provincial printers were crucial to the book trade, since the newspapers they were producing often carried advertisements for London booksellers, and by promoting the circulation of books from the capital they facilitated the development of a bookselling network which came to cover much of the country. The fact that many new roads were being created and many existing roads improved greatly facilitated this development, since transportation of books and materials became swifter and more efficient. Provincial bookselling flourished during the century: there were some 300 booksellers outside London by the 1740s and this increased to around 1,000 by the end of the century. These booksellers were usually not dealing exclusively with books – books were traded alongside other goods, particularly stationery – and the business could be perilous. The father of Samuel Johnson, for example, was a bookseller in Lichfield and endured a continual struggle to keep the business afloat. But basically these were boom years for the book trade – a trade which began to foster some sense of cultural community across Britain's diverse regions. Print enabled people to be better informed about what was going on elsewhere in the country or abroad. Through news, they could feel themselves involved in the politics of the nation, while the availability of the same reading matter to consumers in places as distant as, say, Bristol and Durham, brought far-flung people together as sharers in a common culture.

Print was also, of course, a means of making opinions public and of participation within the world of politics. The presses could be exploited in this way by politicians themselves but also by individuals excluded from direct political engagement who could harness the potential of print to rouse opinion and thereby lobby for particular issues. An early and vivid demonstration of the power of a liberated press to stir up and transmit public opinion came about in 1709 when the Reverend Henry Sacheverell (1674?–1724) preached a controversial sermon implicitly condemning the Glorious Revolution and criticizing the government. In response, the government sought to charge Sacheverell with seditious libel and this caused an intense print war to flare up, as Sacheverell's opponents and supporters endeavoured to intervene in the case. Altogether more than 600 pamphlets, books and sermons relating to the matter were published, and demand for Sacheverell's controversial sermon was huge – it is estimated that around 100,000 copies were produced (O'Gorman 1997, 45). The print war inspired rioting and demonstrations, and although Sacheverell was found guilty, his light sentence – a three-year ban on preaching – was clearly aimed towards appeasing both sides: public support for Sacheverell, spreading because of the presses, could not simply be ignored by the authorities. The Sacheverell case generated great business for the printing industry; at the same time it highlighted the real influence that printed matter could exert within political discourse. And print was to perform that function many times in the years that followed.

The political system and the major political issues

The Sacheverell case, in fact, leads us back to a matter which engrossed many writers of the time – the post-revolutionary political system – for it was fought out in terms of 'Whig' and 'Tory' Party allegiances (of which more later) and as such it was a flash-point in an ongoing rivalry between the political parties which had become increasingly polarized by the new form of government. With the nation governed, as the philosopher John Locke (1632–1704) theorized it, by means of a 'contract' between the king and the people as represented in Parliament, an increasing amount of business became the province of Parliament, while factions and interests within that body became more significant than in previous years. Between 1688 and 1789 those factions, of course, evolved and shifted greatly in response to immediate events, public senti-ment, individual political interests and personalities, as well as the actions of the monarch. The principal opposition between Whigs and Tories was by no means stable and at times, such as during the early reign of George III in the 1760s, it lost much of its significance as a political divide, as new interests and factions came forward. Given these shifting sands, no brief account can provide an explanatory context for individual lit-erary works which responded to or intervened in the politics of the day – they need to be treated on a case by case basis with attention to the specifics of their moment. Nonetheless it will be helpful as a basis for that type of interpretive work to consider some general aspects of the political world and some of the major issues which preoccupied it: the succession, the union of Britain, religion, the growing economy, and Britain's interventions in the wider world.

One novelty of the period was simply *more* parliamentary business. The Bill of Rights stated that regular meetings of Parliament should be a new feature of political life so as to balance the power of the monarch (under the Stuarts there had been long gaps with no parliamentary activity), and prolonged annual sessions became essential when it was decided that gov-ernment funding should be approved by Parliament for a period of just one year. Parliament thus gained control over the economy, and since a principal economic issue in the 25 years following the revolution was the funding of costly wars, it gave Parliament considerable influence over foreign policy.

For a long time, the majority in Parliament supported an aggressive, confrontational approach to European conflict. The belligerent policy pursued by William in the Nine Years' War continued during Queen Anne's reign (1702–14) with the War of the Spanish Succession (1701–14), which saw major victories for Britain under the direction of John Churchill, the first Duke of Marlborough (1650–1722). This was another war fought to curtail the international ambitions of France and the threat of a potentially vast Bourbon empire involving both France and Spain. At the same time, France was posing a danger to Britain itself, with threats to invade and force upon the throne the 'Old Pretender', the Catholic son of James II, thus undoing the work of the revolution. Marlborough's victories over the French meant that in the long term Britain prospered enormously, principally by gaining control over international trade, but in terms of both human lives and money the war was expensive, and in its later phases the campaigns – and Marlborough – came to attract widespread criticism. When Marlborough died, a spectacular attack upon him as a self-interested warmonger was written by Jonathan Swift (1667–1745) in 'A Satirical Elegy On the Death of a Late Famous General'.

The costs of the early wars of this period in fact determined the nature of Britain's national economy for years to come. They were funded through government debt – national borrowing from investors who were repaid with interest from funds raised through taxation. Parliament took responsibility for managing the national debt – it was for this reason that the Bank of England was established in 1694 – and Britain retained its debt and continued mobilizing the resources of investors to pursue further wars and projects throughout the eighteenth century. It was chiefly on this 'mortgaged' economic basis that Britain was able to gain influence over international trade, and to establish the network of colonies which ultimately would be consolidated into the British Empire.

The early years of the post-1689 regime involved a good deal of tentativeness as the monarch and Parliament negotiated their new relationship, but that Parliament had really attained supremacy was made clear in 1701 with the passing of the Act of Settlement, which further limited royal power and reasserted Parliament's role in deciding matters of royal succession. The Act came about when the death of the only child of Princess Anne, William's sister-in-law and heir to the throne, reopened the question of the succession. Faced with a potential crisis, Parliament again secured a Protestant monarchy by legislating that George, Elector of Hanover and great grandson of James I, should follow Anne. In addition, the Act stated that parliamentary consent was required for British participation in wars defending the continental assets of foreign British kings. This was an act of assertion in response to William's military campaigns and of insurance against whatever wars future Hanoverian monarchs might seek to pursue. Britain would accept a German king, but if the country was to go to war, the legislation assured, it must be done in Britain's interests. Both through its consequences and as a symbolic marker, the Act of Settlement was a bold affirmation of the authority of the post-revolutionary system and of the new power of Parliament.

Parliament, though, was by no means a harmonious institution united behind an aim to balance the power of the monarch. Like the people it represented, it was factionalized by disagreement over the economy, the royal ascendancy, religion, foreign policy and other issues. The main opposition of the period between Whigs and Tories emerged from a complex web of conflicts and interests. Tories typically upheld a belief in hereditary royal succession and the divine right of monarchs – so the revolution of 1688–89 left many Tories in a quandary, being obliged to support the monarch, but uneasy about a monarch who had simply been appointed. For those Tories who were unable to approve the line of William, and thereafter the Hanoverian succession, Jacobitism provided an alternative but problematic allegiance – they could support James's bloodline but not his Catholicism – and in fact the Tories were continually associated with Jacobitism throughout the first half of the eighteenth century.

The Tories were also seen as the 'Church party', through their defence of the Anglican Church in a climate of increased tolerance of Protestant nonconformists led by William and the post-revolutionary Whig ministries. Following the passing of a Toleration Act in 1689, Protestant dissenters enjoyed a number of new rights: so long as they swore allegiance to the crown, they were able to set up and gain licences for non-Anglican houses of worship and could run their own schools and academies. The Act did not grant total toleration: dissenters were still debarred from English universities, they could not sit in Parliament, they were excluded from other public offices, and they had to pay tithes to the Anglican Church. And the Act did not grant liberties to Catholics, Jews or followers of other faiths. But it nonetheless posed an important challenge to the established authority of the Anglican Church and was regarded as a serious threat to the nation by many Tories. Exacerbating Tory discontent was the controversial matter of 'Occasional Conformity' – the possibility for dissenters to take Anglican communion once every year so as to gain the same rights as Anglicans to hold public offices. When the Tories gained power, they closed the loophole by passing the Occasional Conformity Act of 1711, but in 1719 the Whig ministry again appealed to dissenters by repealing the act.

With regard to foreign policy, the Whigs were the party which supported Britain's expansionist ambitions overseas, while there was regular Tory criticism of the financial and human cost of the wars fought under William and Anne. The vast majority of Tory and Whig politicians derived their wealth from land – the House of Commons as well as the House of Lords was peopled by the elite – but the Tories came to be the party speaking up for the landed interest, while Whigs were generally sympathetic to new forms of enterprise and commerce not tied to land ownership. Because of the way the wars were funded, it was typically the moneymen who were reaping a profit from their shares in the national debt while landowners felt the brunt of the extra taxes which were levied to keep up with the interest payments. Clearly, then, the revolution and much post-revolutionary policy were in line with Whig sympathies, and in fact Whigs domi-nated the government for most of the period. They were unbreakable during the early Hanoverian reigns of George I (1714–27) and George II (1727–60) – monarchs who partici-pated relatively little in British politics, since their main inter-ests lay in Hanover.

The political union of England and Wales with Scotland, in 1707, strengthened the Whig position. This union was not widely desired, but it served immediate interests on both sides of the border: in England there were fears that Scotland could be used as a base for a French attack and a restoration of the Stuart monarchy, while in Scotland a union offered the prospect of salvation from economic isolation and depres-sion. Scotland's fortunes had been seriously damaged by a failed attempt to set up a colony at Darien in Central America – it was the English, in fact, who had scuppered the scheme, treating Scotland like any other colonial rival. Through the 1707 deal, England agreed to open up her trade to Scotland both domestically and internationally, while Scotland pledged official support for the Hanoverian succes-sion. Scotland also gained an immediate injection of funds as compensation for the long-term responsibility of becom-ing a sharer in the national debt, since a united system of tax-ation was also part of the agreement. The Scottish legal system and the established status of the Presbyterian Church of Scotland, however, remained unchanged. The 1707 union proved to be a turning point in the development of the concept of Britain – an idea that the English, Welsh and Scottish peoples were members of a wider community which arched over the separate regions. This idea was not unknown prior to the official union – the stamping of the figure of Britannia on coins from 1665 is one sign of its earlier circu-lation – but the union injected political reality into that idea, and acted as a catalyst for its development. In terms of par-liamentary politics, an immediate consequence was damage to the strength of the Tories, since the union brought 16 Scottish peers and 45 Scottish commoners into the London Parliament – most of them upholders of Whig policies.

The rivalry between these two parties was at its height in the last years of the reign of Anne, a deeply Anglican queen whose religious convictions were advantageous to the Tories, and this was an era when writers were concertedly engaged in party politics – Swift, for example, was employed to write Tory pamphlets. Increasing opposition to the long war against France, together with the Sacheverell case, led to a Tory administration from 1710 to 1714. At the same time anxiety over Anne's successor generated intense conflict, since despite the Act of Settlement many Tories continued to argue for the greater legitimacy of the Stuart line against the Hanoverian claim. The ultimately smooth accession of George I in 1714 – and the unwillingness of most Tories actively to support the Jacobite rebellion in 1715 – showed that Tories both in Parliament and in the country more widely were prepared to compromise in order to avoid a major armed conflict. Indeed the events of this era have often been seen as a demonstration of the post-revolutionary Parliament's effectiveness as an institution in which conflicts could be resolved – not to the satisfaction of all parties, but without recourse to major violent rebellion or civil war.

Throughout the reigns of the Georges, politicians continued to provide fuel for writers, none more copiously than Robert Walpole (1676–1745), a controversial but resilient statesman who skilfully managed the Whig's dominance of the political scene from 1721 to 1742 (an era often dubbed the 'Robinocracy'). Walpole initially achieved his pre-eminent position through astute financial management, which restored stability after the national chaos caused by the famous 'South Sea Bubble' stock market crash of 1720. This crash occurred when the government allowed a private company, the South Sea Company, to take control of the national debt. When the company's potential was talked up, the value of its stock soared; when the false confidence that had been created collapsed, so did the stock, and many investors faced ruin. Walpole restored order to the country's finances, bringing debt administration back into the government's domain, and thereafter he steered the country through two decades of relative stability, both domestically and on the international scene. As First Lord of the Treasury, Walpole emerged to be the first real 'prime' minister, and he maintained his position with policies which balanced the interests of the landed and mercantile classes. In foreign affairs, he aimed always towards the maintenance of peace and this appeased many Tories, since heavy wartime taxation could be avoided.

Alongside his appeasing policies, Walpole was also an outstandingly talented manipulator of people. His supremacy depended upon slick royal management, initially of George I and, after 1727, of George II and Queen Caroline. When Walpole misjudged the country – as he did in 1733 when his proposal to raise customs and excise duties met with an unexpected and massive uprising of national hostility (an event known as the 'Excise Crisis') – it was largely thanks to George II's support that he was able to survive. Away from the Court, Walpole maintained a network of parliamentary supporters through extensive use of patronage and bribery. Unsurprisingly, Walpole gained a reputation for insincerity and corruption, and as the government made ample use of the press, so too did Walpole's opponents, and some of the century's most distinguished anti-government literature – by, among others, Swift, Alexander Pope (1688–1744), John Gay (1685–1732), and Henry Fielding (1707–54) – emerged from this period. Peachum, the underworld crook in Gay's *The Beggar's Opera* (1728), was just one of numerous veiled portrayals of Walpole as a fraudulent, self-interested manipulator.

The Walpole era drew attention to the corruptibility of politicians and the imperfections of Parliament as a representative body, but many Britons nonetheless felt great pride in their system of government and, compared with their counterparts living under absolutist monarchies on the Continent, they saw themselves as a people enjoying great liberty. 'Lo! Beauteous liberty, the choicest gem / Of Britain's crown', enthused Robert Colvill (d. 1788) in *Britain: A Poem* (1747) (Colvill 1747, 23). Indeed 'liberty' was a catchword associated with Britain throughout the period. Many foreign observers were impressed – the French political theorist, the Baron de Montesquieu (1689–1755), for example, saw in the British system an ideal form of constitutional government.

A key reason for this view of Britain was that Parliament was an *elected* body. Regular elections were inscribed as an essential part of the system of government in the years following the revolution, initially with the Triennial Act of 1694, which made it a requirement that elections be held at least every three years. This was a move to ensure that MPs were removable, and that 'placemen' – subservient followers of the monarch or other interests – could not easily exert long-term influence. In 1716 the term was lengthened to seven years by the Septennial Act, the many elections over the previous two decades having shown that such great frequency was disruptive to parliamentary business. The Jacobite uprising of 1715 also presented a forceful argument for bolstering government stability through longer terms of office. The system of seven years remained in place throughout the period.

Most Britons, in fact, were unable to vote in these elections – that was the privilege of the wealthiest males who held sufficient property to qualify. In the mid-century, around one-fifth of adult males had the right to vote. Yet many non-voters still felt involved in the political system. The press brought people around the country in touch with political events and gave many an opportunity to voice their views; it fostered people's formation of a political identity and a sense of their place and significance within a political domain. And elections were occasions which attracted interest throughout much of the nation and from all quarters: those excluded from the channels of representation could still participate in elections in organizational or lobbying capacities. Furthermore, political awareness spread beyond the capital not only at election time, since many aspects of British life were controlled at the local level, such as the collecting of taxes, military recruitment and, perhaps most importantly, law enforcement – this is why the 'JP', the local Justice of the Peace, looms large in the literature of the period.

Despite the exclusivity of the electoral system, there was no sustained movement for a reform of the franchise during the period. What did attract protest, however, were government actions which appeared to threaten the precious liberties of the people, and in the 1760s a vibrant culture of protest did arise as growing dissatisfaction with the government was mobilized around the figure of John Wilkes (1727–97), a popular radical journalist and MP. By this time, George III, who succeeded his grandfather in 1760, appeared to be asserting the royal prerogative more forcefully than his Hanoverian forebears, and was causing party alliances to dissolve through the appointment of ministers of his choosing – an idea spread that policy was in the hands of a secret cabinet of 'King's Friends'. He was the first of the Georges to take a greater interest in Britain than in Hanover – 'Born and educated in this country I glory in the name of Britain', he famously declared in his first speech to Parliament (Thomas 2002, 33) – and his approach to politics demonstrated that the monarch could still be an influential force, able to grant offices to chosen individuals and to bestow favours, benefits and pensions. His role within government drew criticism: whatever his credentials as a Briton, the king came to be seen by many as a threat to liberty. At the same time, Britain was again being put to the test in a further major war against France, the Seven Years' War (1756–63), fought out on fronts in Europe, India and North America. Under the overall direction of William Pitt (1708–78), a minister backed by widespread popular support, the war turned out remarkably well for Britain and boosted her colonial power enormously, but the country paid dearly for it, and an immediate short-term consequence was a serious economic depression. Further dissatisfaction was created by the fact that, by the end of the war, the king had replaced Pitt with his ex-tutor, the Earl of Bute (1713–92), and had left Bute to negotiate the Treaty of Paris in 1763, which brought peace but alienated Britain from old allies, particularly Prussia.

Wilkes was openly critical of the government, attacking and ridiculing the king and Bute's administration from 1762 in his weekly oppositional paper, the *North Briton*, and later through other publications – the support he garnered was another example of the power of the press. Issue No. 45 of the *North Briton* was especially controversial for its questioning of the honesty of the government, and it became one of the most talked-about publications of the time. The government repeatedly sought to suppress Wilkes. Among other actions taken against him, he was charged with seditious libel, he was expelled from Parliament several times, and the result of an election in which he was the winner was overturned. Responding with defiance, Wilkes soon became a figurehead of protest among the masses – particularly the middling orders – whose backing of causes, including the right to speak out against the government and to publish the truth, became channelled into the vague but emotive general cry of 'Wilkes and liberty!'

George III's handling of government intimated the onset of autocratic rule; the public outpouring of Wilkesite protest showed that such rule would not be quietly tolerated. In the American colonies, where Wilkes also became a popular hero, related dissatisfaction with rigid, unsympathetic British government brought about even greater protests and ultimately led to the War of Independence (1775–83) and the loss of the American colonies – a development which many in Britain saw as a national disaster precipitated by an inept king. In Britain, the immediate Wilkesite protests were contained, but they set in motion a movement for reform which would later come seriously to question why citizens in a land of liberty should be dictated to by a monarch and by statesmen who were in government thanks either to hereditary privilege, if they sat in the House of Lords, or through election by the propertied few.

The social order

The exclusivity of government and of the electoral system was part of a broader pattern of inequality which prevailed in what was a deeply inegalitarian society. Wealth and power were the preserve of a small elite class, and with wealth came numerous advantages which most of the lower orders could only dream of: access to education, better nutrition and health, enjoyment of extensive leisure time, and so on. The primary foundation of wealth was land, and the highest positions in society were for the most part occupied by wealthy landowners. Land provided secure wealth – through rents and farming revenues it supplied a regular income, albeit one subject to fluctuations according to the harvest and agricultural prices. And since land was passed on primarily through inheritance and through marriage, landownership was largely maintained as the preserve of a small and exclusive set comprised firstly of the aristocracy and secondly of the landed gentry. In fact, the terms 'gentry' and 'gentleman' did not have specific, official meanings – people could simply ascribe them to themselves – but they typically referred to those who were descended from peers via younger sons and brothers, and so did not hold titles. With that background, non-titled landowners remained closely connected to the nobility, and often there were marriages which crossed these ranks. In terms of social status, the aristocracy retained a superior claim, but in considering who made up the uppermost stratum of eighteenth-century society, both groups need to be included.

It really was a very small elite group. When Gregory King (1648–1712), an early surveyor of English society, drew up a 'Scheme of the Income and Expense of the Several Families of England . . . for 1688', he identified approximately 3 per cent of the population of five and a half million as members of landowning families (O'Gorman 1997, 14–15). Historians do not accept King's scheme as an entirely accurate picture of the English social structure – indeed most statistics regarding the period need to be treated with great caution since this was, in many ways, a 'pre-statistical' age before accurate figures regarding population and other matters were recorded (the first official national census was in 1801). King's scheme is also limited by its exclusive focus upon England, which ignores the estimated one million Scots, half a million Welsh, and two and a half million living in the Irish colony. Nonetheless, it gives a good impression of a society in which a tiny proportion of the population owned and controlled most of the land – around two-thirds of the owned land, estimates suggest, with much of the remainder being owned by the Church, the Crown and the universities. Landownership was not only the main source of wealth; it was also the basis of numerous powers, rights and privileges, above and beyond the power that fell upon peers through their entitlement to a seat in the House of Lords. Landowners were dominant in central government, in the House of Commons, in the Church, in the officer ranks of the army and navy, in the law, and in local administration.

Land remained the main source of wealth throughout the period, but with the growth of trade, government stocks, manufacturing industries and overseas enterprises, a non-landed class of wealthy businessmen was emerging, and many among the elite feared the rise of these *parvenu* rich and made efforts to maintain the connection between power and land. For example, in 1732 legislation was passed that made it a requirement for Justices of the Peace to be owners of land sufficient to return an annual income of £100 – and this was raised to £300 in the mid-century. Similarly the right to hunt was a privilege exclusive to landowners – this went back to a seventeenth-century law, but revealingly the law was renewed and revised in the eighteenth century. There was, then, significant social tension in the period as commercial conditions opened up possibilities for social mobility based on wealth, since an *arriviste* tradesman or broker could buy the trappings of high rank, while conservatism among the upper class meant that those without land-based wealth or the distinction of lineage were partly excluded from, or only uneasily integrated within elite circles. At the same time, for aristocrats whose fortunes were declining or whose desires outstretched their wealth, the new merchant classes could provide salvation, and there was a healthy marriage market through which those with new money could acquire status while aristocrats could buttress their family fortunes. It is this type of business arrangement that the artist William Hogarth

(1697–1764) famously depicted in *Marriage à-la-Mode* (1743) –
a series of paintings and engravings charting an arranged
marriage going disastrously wrong.

The idea of a 'middle class' did not gain widespread currency until the end of the eighteenth century, with the term
itself coming into general usage in the 1780s. Nonetheless,
from early on contemporaries sometimes saw their society
in terms of a tripartite division. Daniel Defoe (1661?–1731),
for example, has his protagonist/narrator in *Robinson Crusoe*
(1719) describe a 'middle Station of Life' – a position
between 'the Mean and the Great' (Defoe 1994, 5). It is not
completely out of place, then, to think of a middle layer
within eighteenth-century society so long as it is understood
that this category was comprised of people following a vast
variety of professions and occupations, and consequently
with a wide range of incomes and living standards. It was a
category that included many from the agrarian community:
freeholders of land (that is, those who owned the land they
farmed but were not drawing income from renting land)
and tenant farmers (although tenant farmers could also be
very poor). According to Gregory King, families within these
two agricultural groups made up nearly a third of the total
population (O'Gorman 1997, 14–15). Also occupying the
middle ranks were professionals – clergymen, military
officers, lawyers – as well as a growing number of merchants,
small manufacturers, shopkeepers and traders. As Britain
became more consumerist and commercially oriented, the
mushrooming of those numbers working within the mercantile sectors became one of the most striking social transformations of the period. The economist and philosopher,
Adam Smith (1723–90), dubbed Britain 'a nation of shopkeepers' in *The Wealth of Nations* (1776) – long before
Napoleon used the phrase – and by Smith's time retail had
indeed become all the rage, with approximately one shop for
every 35 Britons (Smith 1776, II, 221). The period saw a proliferation of all manner of consumer goods to be traded from
these shops: ceramics, furniture, clothes and other textiles,
and an increasingly diverse range of foodstuffs including

imports from around the world such as coffee, tea, chocolate, sugar, and so on.

Middle-class consumerism was also important to literary production, for the middling orders were becoming avid consumers of printed matter – indeed they were crucial to what might be termed the eighteenth-century emergence of the reading classes. Their growing prosperity meant greater opportunities for education. Britain had no formalized school system, but the importance of education – in independent schools or at home – came to be recognized across a broader range of the social spectrum, and learning became established as an attribute of polite, cultivated identity. There was a marked increase in literacy in the period, particularly among women. It is probable that by 1750 at least 60 per cent of adult males could read – up from around 40 per cent at the beginning of the century. In the same period female literacy doubled from around 20 per cent to around 40 per cent. Increases in literacy needs to be seen as a strand within the complex development of reading culture involving the expansion of the print trade and the emergence of a national network of bookselling. More and more people wanted to experience the communication phenomenon that was burgeoning around them, and learning to read was a way of gaining access to an exciting new culture of print so as both to be entertained and to become better informed about what was going on in the world.

For many among the middling ranks, growing prosperity also brought increasing leisure time, and this too fuelled literary culture and affected its development. For example, the novel, a genre which many argue was truly born in the eighteenth century, is a form which demands *time*. The growing popularity of novels was dependent upon a body of readers not only with the resources to buy or borrow reading matter – subscription libraries were another new feature on the eighteenth-century cultural landscape – but also the leisure time required to consume long, multi-volume works. A mammoth novel such as *Clarissa* (1747–48) by Samuel Richardson (1689–1761) would almost certainly not have been written had there not been a community of potential readers able to devote extensive time – in the case of *Clarissa*, possibly several weeks – to literary consumption.

While Britain was becoming more literate, there remained a significant proportion of the population who could not read, and for the most part this mapped onto the large numbers making up the labouring classes and the poor, although there were some within those groups who could read and write. Agricultural labourers, household servants, workers in small manufactories, urban labourers and so on were typically rewarded with extremely low wages. And if they found themselves unable to work, there was no national system of support to help them: those who could not earn a living due to age or infirmity were usually dependent upon the goodwill of relatives or others in order to survive. Poor relief could be granted by a parish, but charity was not available to all and paupery was common. Disease presented a constant threat. This was a threat, of course, to all classes. Alongside an array of individual ailments, Britons had good reason to fear a repeat of the Great Plague of 1665 – not least in the 1720s when the plague was ravaging the south of France. The plague did not return to Britain, but there were devastating epidemics of influenza and smallpox, and while the period saw advancements in medical knowledge and practice, treatments were still relatively primitive. And they were mostly unavailable to the poor, whose vulnerability to disease was often compounded by unsanitary living conditions and meagre nutrition.

Crime was one way in which the poor might try to improve their lot, and Britain's increasingly materialist culture saw a marked increase in crimes against property, particularly following poor harvests or at the conclusion of a war when disbanded soldiers returned to their homeland with no way of making a legal living. London presented the greatest opportunities for crime, and remarkably sophisticated criminal networks developed there – it is in the milieu of London's organized crime that John Gay set his *Beggar's Opera*. But an increase in crime occurred countrywide. In response, the government made criminal punishments more severe, among other measures increasing the number of crimes punishable by death – executions, usually by hanging, were still carried out in public and would often draw large crowds. By 1800 around 200 crimes carried the death penalty, many of them property crimes. Such changes to the justice system reflected the revered status of private property – in an era when there were more and more goods around – as the authorities strove to teach that rights of ownership must be respected. The harshness of criminal law did not go unnoticed. In Henry Fielding's *Joseph Andrews* (1742), for example, Joseph is charged with stealing a hazel twig while his companion is charged with aiding and abetting – it is a satirical episode in a novel which repeatedly draws attention to the divide between rich and poor.

Social divisions were so marked in the period that it was inevitable that countless authors should explore the stratification of their society in their works and exploit the narrative possibilities it presented. Class differentiation could provide the basis of great tension, as in Richardson's tale of cross-class seduction in *Pamela* (1740–42), and also of comedy, as in *She Stoops to Conquer* (1773) by Oliver Goldsmith (1728–74), where a drama of pretence and disguise makes light of the outward signs of class while also showing how deeply such signs could penetrate human consciousness, and actually determine actions and inner feelings. Social position hung upon wealth and background but, as Goldsmith's play suggests, it was also something to be *performed*: modes of dress, wigs, deportment, gestures, ways of speaking – all such codes gave individuals a means of displaying their position in public. At the same time, there was a growing attention to moral conduct as a mark of true social status. The expansion of the middle classes was concomitant with the growth of a powerful moral reform movement and great energy was expended upon defining proper conduct and correcting existing vices. Such reform gained an institutional basis in the 'Society for the Reformation of Manners', founded in 1690, and further organizations were established with a view to suppressing profanity, sexual depravity and other perceived vices. In fact, Richardson's *Pamela* is in part a conduct manual – as a tale of an upper-class rake's reformation, it is a middle-class endeavour to display patterns of moral behaviour from which all classes might learn.

Inequality shaped gender relations as well as those of class. It was a fiercely patriarchal society, in which women were accorded secondary status both through prevailing attitudes and through the law. Financial independence was denied to most women due to restrictions on their rights to own property: a married woman's property came under the control of her husband, and property would be passed on through sons before it could be inherited by a daughter. And many areas of public life were closed to women: for example, they could not vote, and were debarred any direct role in politics. A few women were in a position to influence politicians or the monarch, but they were excluded from direct power. However, some women were able to achieve successful careers in certain male-dominated areas, including the world of learning, the theatre, and imaginative literature. In fact, it was a good time for female authors who, following Aphra Behn (1640–89) – seen by many as the first female 'professional author' whose living derived from writing – seized the new opportunities presented by the explosion of print and, through skill and determination, managed to carve out careers as authors. But these women were the exceptions and most operated within spheres of opportunity which were far more constrained than those of men.

Regarding sexual practice, a firm double standard was upheld, and this, like so much else, was tied up with property, as well as with the maintenance of the nuclear family which was the basic building-block of British society. Clear chains of ownership and the unity of a family were seen to depend upon the preservation of female chastity until marriage, and of monogamy after marriage. 'Confusion of progeny constitutes the essence of the crime', Samuel Johnson observed of adultery, 'and therefore a woman who breaks her marriage vows is much more criminal than a man who does it. A man, to be sure, is criminal in the sight of God: but he does not do his wife a very material injury, if . . . he steals privately to her chambermaid' (Boswell 1980, 393–4). Pregnancy outside of wedlock carried great shame for women, and bastard children were often viewed with contempt, and treated with hostility.

As with the social hierarchy, the inequality of the sexes was widely assumed to be the natural order of the world. The period saw nothing that could really be described as a feminist 'movement'. However, there were isolated voices which protested about the position of women, and some of these found their way into print – for example, Mary Collier (c. 1690–1762), a washerwoman and amateur poet who wrote vividly of the drudgery of domestic labour, and, at the other end of the class scale, Lady Mary Wortley Montagu (1689–1762), an intellectual and wit who, while not aiming to publish, wrote bold complaints about women's educational opportunities and responded to hostile and misogynistic verses by Swift and Pope with vigorous poetic ripostes. By the 1780s, a more rigorous feminist agenda was beginning to be put together by Mary Wollstonecraft (1759–97), but, as with the social order, sexual inequalities within Britain were not radically challenged in any organized or sustained way during our period. Indeed, many believed that inequality on earth was inherent to human existence and was sanctioned by God – that men and women were positioned within a 'chain of being', stretching from God himself at the top, down through the layers of human society and into the animal kingdom. Questioning one's place within that structure, such thinking went, would be an offence against divine purpose.

RELIGION, SCIENCE AND PHILOSOPHY

Faith and religious observance

Christian belief ran deep through eighteenth-century society, as the bitter conflicts surrounding the succession of the monarch boldly demonstrated early on in the period. Consequently, Christian doctrine provided a framework for numerous literary works – often only implicitly, when Christian explanations of the way of things were simply assumed as shared ground between an author and his or her readers. Most Britons believed that God was the creative power behind the universe, and the period's theological disputes and tensions typically concerned the nature and practice of religion rather than any widespread questioning of the existence of God, as would occur in the atheistic movements of the nineteenth century.

As we have seen, the post-revolutionary granting of rights to Protestant dissenters provoked fierce disagreements between Whigs and Tories, and this was in part because the legitimization of dissent could be regarded not only as a religious issue, but also as a threat to the authority of one of the main structuring institutions of society. The land was organized around the churches. The parishes of the Church of England, of which there were some 10,000, were the basic units into which the country was divided, and the role of the Church stretched beyond the spiritual needs of parishioners and into local administration, law-keeping, the organization of poor relief, and so on. And since parishioners were expected to attend church regularly, the Church was seen to be a valuable agent of social cohesion. Early opponents of the Toleration Act, therefore, were concerned not only for the fate of the Church but for the stability of society in general. Uniting around a cry of 'The Church in Danger', many were genuinely fearful of national turmoil, not least since the middle years of the seventeenth century had already provided a frightening example of the social and political turbulence that could be caused by religious factionalism and fanaticism. The established Church, though, did not lose its privileged position, and while religious tensions persisted, most Anglicans were able to compromise and to live relatively harmoniously alongside the Presbyterians (the largest dissenting group), Baptists, Congregationalists, Quakers and other Protestant nonconformists. With Presbyterianism remaining the established religion in Scotland after the 1707 union, the new nation was, at least within its Protestant bounds, unusually pluralist. And the relative freedom of worship enjoyed by Britons – a privilege which seemed to be all the more liberally granted when the more stringent religious systems in place across much of Europe were considered – became another aspect of society in which champions of British liberty could take great pride.

Catholics, Jews and other non-Protestants, of course, could not share in this sense of freedom, and had good reason to wonder about the nature of Britain's religious 'tolerance'. Hostility towards Catholicism – or 'popery' as it was commonly called – was widespread, and was actually something around which Anglicans and nonconformist Protestants could unite. Catholics were subject by law to severe civil restrictions: Alexander Pope, for example, was a Catholic, and as such was not allowed to attend university, to hold a public office, to own land or to vote. Irish Catholics were similarly discriminated against, and Britain's firm government of Ireland during the period was maintained with a view to keeping the Catholic majority under control. On top of official discrimination, there was a good deal of public hostility to Catholics – often tied up with patriotic sentiment and opposition to France, especially during the many years when Britain was at war with her Catholic neighbour. In fact the British people proved to be more intolerant than their government. In 1778 a Roman Catholic Relief Act was passed which allowed Catholics to participate in public life (conveniently for the government, it also allowed them to join the army, which at the time was in need of recruits), but the Act met with a massive demonstration of popular opposition. A movement to repeal the Act was headed by Lord George Gordon (1751–93), whose campaigning led to the so-called 'Gordon Riots' of 1780 which for a time threw London into a state of chaos and lawlessness. The riots cannot be attributed purely to anti-Catholicism – as with the earlier Wilkesite protests, unrest at this time grew out of a constellation of popular grievances – but anti-Catholicism provided the touch-paper.

Like Catholics, Jews were punitively sidelined within British society and were widely regarded with intolerance. In the mid-century there was an attempt to improve the civil status of Jews when a Jewish Naturalization Act (often known as the 'Jew Bill') was passed through Parliament in 1753, but the Act met with such harsh opposition – particularly from high-Church Anglicans – that the government was forced to repeal it in order not to lose support. The extent of Britain's religious tolerance, then, clearly depended upon the position from which it was viewed.

While other faiths tended to meet hostility from the Anglican establishment, many Anglican churchmen held relatively open-minded, pragmatic attitudes when it came to the manner in which their parishioners should observe their Christianity. The early years of the period saw heated and very public theological debates around the competing claims of 'revealed religion' and 'rational religion' (or 'deism'). In 'revealed religion' the workings of God are believed to be seen in supernatural events such as miracles, and the institution of the Church is treated as a true channel of divine authority. In contrast, 'rational religion' rejects the idea of supernatural manifestations of God and the divine authority of the Church, and rather bases belief upon human reason. Rational religion finds evidence for God's existence in, for example, the natural world – in things which can be humanly observed – and it found a radical proponent in the controversial figure of Benjamin Hoadly (1676–1761), a Bishop of Bangor who, despite his position within the established Church, argued that organized religion was basically irrelevant since faith was at heart a matter between an individual and God. Hoadly made his views well known – indeed in 1717 he preached them before George I and sparked off a storm of disagreement between churchmen and politicians (known as the 'Bangorian Controversy'). Hoadly occupied an extreme low-Church position – and became deeply unpopular among churchmen because of it – but less radical low-Church attitudes gained considerable ground within Anglicanism, not least since Whig politicians took steps to promote low-Church clerics to the highest ecclesiastical offices. It became common, therefore, for eighteenth-century clergy to downplay the mysteries of divinity in favour of 'practical religion', and to promote a manner of observance which emphasized the individual's adherence to the codes of Christian virtue and the performance of good works over the actual issue of faith itself (although it was, of course, assumed that a Christian would have that faith).

A different approach to religious observance was found in Methodism, the period's foremost evangelical movement which began to attract adherents from the 1740s onwards after its foundation by a group of students at Oxford including the main leader, John Wesley (1703–91) and his brother Charles Wesley (1707–88). Methodists reacted against the low-Church approach to faith and to what they saw as apathy and complacency within the Anglican Church. Anglican preachers, in fact, had gained a reputation for being uninspiring, and were often criticized and mocked on the grounds of dullness – Hogarth, for example, satirized Anglican oratory and its effects in an engraving called 'The Sleeping Congregation' (1736). For the Methodists, poor preachers were abusing their position as agents of God, and were failing in their duty to spread true religion. As an alternative, Methodists sought to fire up their congregations – usually gathered in the open air – with oratory aimed at inspiring feelings of the 'New Birth'. Such preaching certainly attracted interest – one of the leaders of the movement, George Whitefield (1714–70), became renowned for the vehemence and theatricality of his oratory and for his ability to pull a crowd and hold its attention. And Methodists attracted a significant number of converts and followers – particularly in rural areas and among the poor. Indeed the movement was sufficiently successful to inspire fear within the established Church as well as a lively culture of anti-Methodism, in which Methodists were charged with fanaticism and 'enthusiasm' (a false belief of divine possession) and with undermining the structures and cohesion of society.

The divisions within Britain's religious culture, then, were a cause of ongoing disagreement and unrest. Large-scale conflict between religious groups was avoided, but, as is reflected in many contemporary literary works – such as Swift's *A Tale of a Tub* (1704) which allegorizes Catholic, Anglican and Dissenting approaches to faith – religious diversity proved to be a cause of continual tension.

Scientific exploration and innovation

Faith also lay behind much of the exploratory thought and scientific investigation of the period. The hero of the time within science – or 'natural philosophy', as it was known – was Isaac Newton (1642–1727), whose theories and discoveries revolutionized the fields of optics, mathematics, astronomy and physics. Offering explanations of the nature of light, of gravity, of planetary motion and other natural phenomena, Newton was seen to have penetrated further than anyone before him into the workings of the universe – as Pope put it in a famous epitaph for Newton, 'Nature and Nature's laws lay hid in night, / God said, *Let Newton be!* And all was light' (Pope 1735, II, 170). Pope's biblical allusion here is very fitting, for Newton's science was theistic: his work assumed that the mechanisms of the universe were open to rational analysis and explanation, but he could not explain the actual existence of the universe as anything other than the remarkable work of God. The universe, to apply a common analogy for such thinking, was like a watch with God as the watchmaker: science could explore the interrelated parts and actions that allowed the watch to function; it could not explain why the watch had been made, but the existence of a maker had to be assumed.

Newton's work, then, was both theistic and deeply *empiricist* – that is, his conclusions were drawn upon the basis of what could be observed and experienced – and this orientation was found in much eighteenth-century science. As with rational religion, many thinkers believed that the best way to get to know God was by gathering knowledge of his creation.

Pope can be called upon again here, for he provided a succinct expression of this attitude in his *Essay on Man* (1733–34):

> Say first, of God above, or Man below,
> What can we reason, but from what we know?
> Of Man what see we, but his station here,
> From which to reason, or to which refer?
> Through worlds unnumbered though the God be known,
> 'Tis ours to trace him only in our own.
> (Pope 2006, 272)

Aside from demonstrating how poetry, at this time, was seen as a perfectly suitable medium for engaging in intellectual debate (about which more will be said in the next chapter), the passage encapsulates the commonly held view that study of 'our own' world should be favoured over metaphysical speculation. This empiricism was not new in the period: it had already been significantly advanced through the scientific work of Francis Bacon (1561–1626), author of the seminal empiricist treatise, *The Advancement of Learning* (1605). An empiricist approach also underlay the early experiments and publications of the Royal Society – a group of scientists who met informally from the 1640s and whose work gained official endorsement soon after the 1660 Restoration when Charles II chartered 'The Royal Society of London for Improving Natural Knowledge'. In the eighteenth century, though, empiricism became more and more orthodox within intellectual enquiry, and it was a period during which experimentation and exploration truly flourished.

Exploration took many forms. The most daring was that which sought to study the world beyond the little patch of northern Europe that was known to most Britons. Naval expertise had long been one of the country's most valuable assets: wars were won and lucrative colonies were established because of English shipping skills, and the mass trading of goods from around the world depended upon the efficiency of Britain's fleet. Britain's international commerce included, of course, the trading of slaves, and vast numbers of enslaved

West Africans were transported on British ships to the American colonies and Caribbean before the trade was abolished in 1807. But ships were also used for less barbarous causes, as explorers undertook ambitious voyages of global discovery. It was in this period, for example, that Captain James Cook (1728–79) made his three voyages to the South Pacific, charting for the first time the contours of little-known and newly discovered lands, and making observations of their inhabitants, while the botanist Joseph Banks (1743–1820) made studies of flora and fauna quite unknown to Europeans. Such voyages were rarely completely free from commercial motives, but a priority was the empirical pursuit of knowledge. And the British public was clearly keen to learn the results of these exploratory travels, for published accounts of exotic journeys, with their promise of opening new horizons of awareness, proved perennially popular within the market for print.

But there was also much that could be discovered without boarding ship. The Royal Society, of which Newton was the president from 1703 until his death in 1727, continued to foster a culture of experimentation and technical innovation – a culture which spread beyond the scientific elite to encompass many amateur scientists and 'projectors'. At the same time, the refinement of scientific instruments, such as the telescope and the microscope, was opening up new spheres of knowledge and new ways of thinking about the world and human life. Major advances in microscopy, for instance, had earlier been made by Robert Hooke (1635–1703), Curator of Experiments at the Royal Society, who published his results in *Micrographia; or, Some physiological descriptions of minute bodies made by magnifying glasses* (1665). This work included meticulously engraved illustrations of, for example, snowflakes and a flea – images exhibiting details of these tiny objects quite impossible to detect with the naked eye. Was it possible, people began to wonder in response to such revelations, that there were minute worlds and universes existing within the world they knew? And could it be, as telescopic investigations of the solar system and beyond might suggest, that the Earth was itself just a tiny world within a living system of creation far vaster than people had imagined? Optical instruments produced a sense of wonder regarding the possibilities of what was not known. Joseph Addison (1672–1719) marvelled at the discoveries 'made by Glasses', which could suggest that 'every green Leaf swarm[ed] with Millions of Animals, that at their largest Growth are not visible to the naked Eye'. He felt 'a pleasing Astonishment, to see so many Worlds hanging one above another', and in contemplating that 'in the smallest Particle of this little World' there might be 'a new inexhausted Fund of Matter, capable of being spun out into another Universe' (Bond 1965, III, 574–6). And such science posed a challenge to the view that human life and the familiar world were the high achievements of God's creation. A rethinking of the 'chain of being' emerges, for example, in Gulliver's discovery of minute and giant lands in Swift's *Gulliver's Travels*, a work in which the idea that humankind's importance may be relative to that of other beings serves as a basis for a critique of human pride.

Gulliver's Travels, in fact, includes cutting satire of aspects of Britain's scientific culture. The Royal Society's sponsoring of experiments of all kinds is lampooned, for instance, in Swift's representations of a scientist pursuing 'a Project for extracting Sunbeams out of Cucumbers' and of an 'ingenious Architect who had contrived a new Method for building Houses, by beginning at the Roof and working downwards to the Foundation' (Swift 2001, 167–8). But while Swift mocked many forms of experiment as *outré* and extravagant, he was happy to promote scientific innovation when it was clearly directed to bettering the general lot of mankind – as he has one of his characters observe: 'whoever could make two Ears of Corn, or two Blades of Grass to grow upon a spot of Ground where only one grew before, would deserve better of Mankind, and do more essential Service to his Country than the whole Race of Politicians put together' (Swift 2001, 126). Such a view was widely held, and alongside the growth of 'pure' science, there was increasing faith in science as a means towards the improvement of human conditions, and the period saw significant innovation and invention within many fields of applied science, including medicine, agriculture and the various branches of engineering.

There was widespread experimentation with new farming techniques, and this made agriculture increasingly efficient. Farmers experimented with new crop-rotation systems, so as to improve the fertility of the soil; new animal husbandry and breeding techniques were developed, resulting in, for example, new strains of sheep and pigs which would fatten up more quickly than previously existing breeds. And new types of farm machinery came into use: more effective ploughs and harrows, and of particular significance towards the end of the period, a revolutionary threshing machine, invented in the 1780s. It was not only experiment and innovation which was transforming British agriculture: a radical reshaping of the land was also occurring through the ongoing (and controversial) process of 'enclosure', whereby parliamentary 'Enclosure Acts' allowed small plots of land to be rationalized into larger units, and areas of common land to be brought under private ownership. Enclosure in itself increased efficiency, but science also made a major contribution to agriculture becoming markedly more productive and less labour intensive: in 1700 just under half of the population worked within agriculture; this dropped to around a third in 1800. In fact, falling demand for labour on the land is one of the reasons why Britain's towns and cities were expanding – the extended consequences of scientific innovation were extremely far-reaching. It is worth noting also here the significance of the printing industry to these changes, for print enabled agricultural innovation to become a country-wide phenomenon – the results of, say, a new crop-rotation system could be published and read by landowners throughout Britain, while new machinery could be widely advertised through the press.

This agricultural revolution facilitated the industrial developments of the following century, but important foundations for later growth had also been laid within the field of engineering. For instance, steam power was developed early in the period by Thomas Newcomen (1663–1729), who invented an engine which could be put to various uses – for example, to pump water out of mines. Newcomen's designs were later worked on and refined by the Scottish engineer James Watt (1736–1819), resulting in a more workable and efficient source of industrial power, and Watt's engines were beginning to come into use towards the end of our period.

There were also important mechanical achievements on a smaller, finer scale. Among the foremost practical scientific problems of the eighteenth century was the question of how to establish the longitudinal position of a ship at sea. This was crucial for accurate navigation which had become a priority for a maritime nation increasingly involved in the wider world through trade, wars, exploration and colonial expansion. So pressing was the problem that the British government set up a Longitude Board, and in 1714 Parliament passed a Longitude Act offering a colossal reward of £20,000 to anyone who could solve the problem. A key difficulty with measuring longitude was that no chronometer existed which would keep accurate time over the course of a sea voyage – with all the movements of a ship, and changes of climate – and the most successful of the numerous projectors to take up Parliament's challenge was John Harrison (1693–1776), an exceptionally gifted horologist who created a series of pioneering clocks and watches, refining the technology of time with each new model.

Harrison devoted most of his life to solving the longitude problem, and his career vividly reflects a burgeoning eighteenth-century faith in modernity and in the possibility of progress through technological innovation. He was arguably an unlikely scientific pioneer. The son of a Yorkshire carpenter, he received no formal education and never gained a real aptitude for writing. In this respect, though, Harrison's work also demonstrates how widely – both socially and geographically – a culture of exploration and invention had spread during the period. In fact, as a low-born artisan Harrison did come into conflict with establishment scientists, including members of the Longitude Board, but despite this he was able to make an extremely significant contribution to the period's new technology, as were many other enterprising inventors and engineers from the lower orders – James Hargreaves (*c.* 1720–78), for example, whose invention of the 'spinning jenny' transformed the textile industry.

Science also became a pursuit for many of the more leisured members of the middle and upper orders of society. Among the majority from these classes who were not actually engaged in scientific work, *knowing about* the latest discoveries and inventions was becoming a sign of polite identity, both for men and for women. Lectures on scientific topics became popular, as did demonstrations of new scientific instruments. For example, James Ferguson (1710–76), a Scottish astronomer, became a popular lecturer among the polite classes with demonstrations of planetary motion, illustrated by means of mechanical orreries and astronomical clocks. It was lectures by popular scientists like Ferguson that were depicted by Joseph Wright of Derby (1734–97) in his well-known paintings 'A Philosopher Giving that Lecture on the Orrery in which a Lamp is put in place of the Sun' (1766) and 'An Experiment on a Bird in the Air Pump' (1768). Ferguson and others also published popular books and pamphlets on scientific subjects as the print trade responded to polite interests in science. Women readers were pointedly targeted by such volumes as *Sir Isaac Newton's Philosophy Explain'd for the Use of Ladies* (1739), a work translated from Italian by Elizabeth Carter (1717–1806), and by periodicals such as the *Female Spectator* by Eliza Haywood (1693–1756). Haywood specifically recommended that women should study science. She included, for example, a long account of a visit to an observatory in order to show her female readers 'how much Pleasure, as well as Improvement, would accrue to them by giving some few Hours, out of the many which they have to spare, to the Study of Natural Philosophy' (Haywood 1745, III, 318). And for Haywood, as for Newton, the theistic basis of science was strong, as the extraordinary observations made through telescopes provided her with 'such a Variety

of Proofs of the Ingenuity God has bestowed on Man'
(Haywood 1745, III, 309).

Explorations in thought

As with science, much eighteenth-century philosophical work
was empiricist and based upon faith. As will have become
clear, there are very few neat boundaries between the period's
theological, scientific and philosophical projects, and the man
who became the eighteenth century's most influential thinker,
John Locke, displayed a typical breadth of interest and commitment in his enquiries into religion, human psychology,
political philosophy and educational theory. Locke died in
1704, but his works were widely reprinted throughout the
century and his ideas remained influential within intellectual
culture. As a theologian, Locke contributed significantly to
the debates over 'rational religion' and 'revealed religion' with
The Reasonableness of Christianity (1695), which offered a succinct articulation of the idea of faith founded on rational
observation, while in his best-known work, *An Essay Concerning
Human Understanding* (1689), he revolutionized conceptions of
human psychology.

Empiricism is at the core of the argument in Locke's *Essay*,
which seeks to explain the nature of human understanding
and to overturn the view that understanding arises from anything *innate*. For Locke, humankind has no innate ideas; rather,
the human mind starts out in the world as a *tabula rasa* – a
blank canvas which becomes marked and formed through
experience. Human understanding, for Locke, is the result of
what is gathered up via the senses during the course of life –
it is the outcome of a type of sensory empirical journey.
This was a radical argument, but Locke's *Essay* came to be
widely accepted and to have a major impact upon the way in
which people considered their own identities to be constituted.
The ideas it advanced also informed the work of many writers
of literature. It can be broadly argued, for example, that
Lockean thought provided an intellectual framework and an
impetus for the proliferation of novels, which typically chart

the growth of characters as they undergo a range of different experiences. Leading characters in novels are rarely introduced fully fledged and then set in motion through a plot; they are rather shown *developing* – being formed through the experience of the incidents and challenges which a novelist might put in their way.

Locke, though, was not only interested in *explaining* human psychology. Like other rational theologians who emphasized the value of 'good works' over faith alone, and like the scientists who sought to apply their discoveries for the benefit of society, Locke was interested in how his thinking could be turned into useful social practice. He applied his ideas of human understanding, for example, to the field of pedagogy in another influential work, *Some Thoughts concerning Education* (1693), and he explored systems of proper political authority in his *Two Treatises of Government* (1689). Indeed he was explicit regarding the practical emphasis of his work. 'Our Business here is not to know all Things', he wrote in the *Essay*, 'but those Things which concern our Conduct. If we can find out those Measures, whereby a rational Creature . . . may and ought to govern his Opinions and Actions depending thereon, we need not be troubled that some other Things escape our Knowledge' (Locke 1721, I, 4).

In fact, the issue of 'our Conduct' – an issue concerning the nature of humankind's sociability and what it means to behave with virtue – remained a preoccupation within eighteenth-century philosophical enquiry. Views of mankind's sociable potential diverged radically. In circulation throughout the period – but by no means universally welcomed – were the ideas of Thomas Hobbes (1588–1679), the author of *Leviathan* (1651), who had earlier put forward a powerful case for the fundamentally self-interested nature of man. For Hobbes, all people are by nature warlike, brutish and primarily concerned with self-preservation and gain. They are able, however, to co-exist in basically peaceable societies by submitting to a 'social contract' – an agreement between the rulers and the ruled which establishes the duties and rights of individuals. Society, for Hobbes, is anarchy held at bay by authority.

A similarly pessimistic view of mankind's natural state was put forward by Bernard de Mandeville (1670–1733), a Dutchman who settled in England where, after mastering the language, he stoked philosophical controversies with his *The Fable of the Bees* (1714–29). Like Hobbes, Mandeville saw mankind as naturally selfish and avaricious, but he proffered the paradoxical argument that such qualities actually served the common good. Subtitling his work *Private Vices Publick Benefits*, he described his aim as 'to demonstrate, That Human Frailties, *during the degeneracy of* Mankind, may be turn'd to the Advantage of the Civil Society, and made to Supply the Place of *Moral Virtues*' (Mandeville 1714, title-page). For Mandeville, a private vice such as greed was socially beneficial for it generated enterprise and wealth among those called upon to satisfy the greedy individual's desires.

The bleak views of humanity which underlay Hobbes's and Mandeville's interpretations of how societies could function and prosper attracted many critics – not least among clergy-men – and they contributed to the emergence of an influen-tial counter-movement within philosophy based upon an alternative view of mankind as fundamentally moral and sym-pathetic. An initiator here was Anthony Ashley Cooper, the third Earl of Shaftesbury (1671–1713), who developed the idea of mankind's 'moral sense' in his *Characteristicks of Men, Manners, Opinions, Times*, first published in 1711 and frequently reprinted throughout the century. The 'moral sense', for Shaftesbury, is a human propensity to *feel* what is virtuous and what is not – to be able to distinguish between the rightness or wrongness of a thought or action according to the involuntary emotional response it engenders. Shaftesbury's optimistic view of human nature attracted many followers – his thinking proved particularly influential within Scottish philosophical circles, where Francis Hutcheson (1694–1746), David Hume (1711–76) and Adam Smith made further contributions to a growing 'moral sense' school of philosophy. Operating with the basic theory that humans are fundamentally social and benevolent, these thinkers are widely credited with having supplied a philosophical basis for the emergence, around the mid-century, of a widespread culture of 'sensibility' – a culture which promoted and celebrated sympathetic actions and the exercise of feeling.

This culture also generated an important new word – 'sentimental' – which would be much used in the latter half of the century, and not in the sense of 'mawkish' or 'excessively emotional' as it is now generally understood. The root of this term, 'sentiment', referred to a thought generated by or involving emotion; it suggested a 'mental feeling' – something which is at once intellectual and emotional, and typically concerned with moral conduct. It is in this sense that Adam Smith used the term in his *Theory of Moral Sentiments* (1759), which develops the idea that proper conduct in society depends upon the exercise of sympathy for one's fellow beings. Anything which could generate sentiments, then, could be dubbed 'sentimental', and this new adjective was also applied to people to suggest their 'sensibility' – their capacity to feel sympathy for others and, by extension, their desire to alleviate the suffering of others. Not everyone was at ease with this newly minted word. John Wesley, for example, complained in 1772 that 'sentimental' 'conveys no determinate idea', but he could not deny that what he found to be a 'nonsensical word' was 'becoming a fashionable one' (Brissenden 1974, 106). Wesley was responding here to the use of the term by Laurence Sterne in a popular work of fiction, *A Sentimental Journey through France and Italy* (1768), in which a whole story is constructed around a character who is obsessed with exercising and examining his feelings. *A Sentimental Journey*, in fact, was one of a great many literary works which participated in what became a widespread cultural phenomenon.

Sentimentalism influenced all genres of literature, as well as painting and music, and, for some decades at least, it had a significant impact upon social behaviour, as individuals sought opportunities to display the fineness of their inner sensibilities. As the author of an article from 1796 recalled, there was a time 'when sensibility was taken under the patronage of that powerful arbiter of manners – fashion. Then, height of breeding was measured by delicacy of feeling, and no fine lady, or gentleman, was ashamed to be seen sighing over a pathetic story, or weeping at a deep-wrought tragedy' (Anon., 1796, 706). Sensibility additionally found less self-indulgent forms of expression, and can be seen to have played a part in charitable projects such as the provision of relief for paupers and the establishment of homes for orphans, foundlings and penitent prostitutes. It also contributed to the growth of the abolitionist movement which ultimately would lead to the end of the British slave trade.

The sentimental phenomenon is a good example of how movements within philosophy came to play a part within different forms of cultural expression and within social practice. Philosophy was not the sole fountainhead of sentimentalism, but thinkers within the 'moral sense' school provided an important intellectual framework for the sympathy-based model of social relations which was central to the movement, and many of their writings became well known and much discussed, for they typically aspired to present their ideas in forms which were accessible to a broad reading public. From early on in the century, individuals interested in shaping society had sought to establish a place for philosophy within general public discourse. In 1711 Joseph Addison wrote of his ambition 'to have it said of me, that I have brought Philosophy out of Closets and Libraries, Schools and Colleges, to dwell in Clubs and Assemblies, at Tea-Tables, and in Coffee-Houses' (Bond 1965, I, 44). David Hume similarly sought to introduce greater learning into the 'conversible World', by which he meant those people who 'join to a sociable Disposition, and a Taste of Pleasure, an Inclination to the easier and more gentle Exercises of the Understanding' (Hume 1742, II, 1), and he noticed in his own time a strengthening 'League betwixt the learned and conversible Worlds' (Hume 1742, II, 4). Philosophy was becoming established as a component of 'polite learning' – at a time when refined pleasures of many kinds were claiming increasing cultural space.

ARTS AND CULTURE

The arts and connoisseurship

The buoyancy of Britain's economy, together with the growth in the number of people with time to devote to the pursuit of pleasure, led to major investment in the arts in the eighteenth century. And as individuals aspired to be identified as members of the polite classes and sought ways to demonstrate their refinement, increasing emphasis was placed upon ideas of artistic taste and connoisseurship. Indeed, within a cultural scene which remained deeply variegated and accommodating of all sorts of production – classicist and modern, imported and vernacular – this movement to demarcate a realm of refined culture was one of the most striking developments of the period. It did not happen immediately after the revolution of 1688. Jonathan Richardson (1665–1745), a prominent portraitist and art theorist, was complaining that Britain lacked lovers and connoisseurs of painting some 30 years after William took the throne. Richardson's *A Discourse on the Dignity, Certainty, Pleasure and Advantage, of the Science of a Connoisseur* (1719) is a plea for a general refinement of the appreciation of painting. But a widespread interest in the arts – and in codes of artistic taste and appreciation – did take hold in Britain. Half a century after Richardson's discourse, Thomas Martyn (1735–1825), the author of *The English Connoisseur: Containing An Account of Whatever is Curious in Painting, Sculpture, &c. In the Palaces and Seats of the Nobility and Principal Gentry of England, Both in Town and Country* (1766), was able to write of the 'great progress which the polite arts have lately made in England, and the attention which is now paid them by almost all ranks of men' (Martyn 1766, i). The idea of proper artistic appreciation as an attribute of polite identity had become established – and it added a thick gloss of virtue to the consumption and enjoyment of an array of cultural pleasures that had become available by that time.

This rise in the value of connoisseurship was in part a consequence of the Grand Tour – a form of refined travel which was increasingly being seen as the proper way to finish the education of a gentleman (or sometimes, but far less frequently, of a lady). There was no set path for these tours, but for young travellers from the affluent classes it became more or less *de rigueur* to pass through a good number of Europe's major cultural centres; there were often erotic pleasures and other kinds of bonus to be found along the way, but cultural refinement was integral to the *idea* of the experience. For Thomas Nugent (*c.* 1700–72), the author of a Grand Tour guidebook, travelling had the capacity 'to enrich the mind with knowledge, to rectify the judgment, to remove the prejudices of education, to compose the outward manners, and in a word to form the complete gentleman' (Nugent 1756, I, xi). To ensure that such ends were pursued, tutors were often employed to accompany the young gentlemen – to direct them towards essential attractions, such as the ruins of ancient Rome and the Renaissance art and architecture of the great Italian cities, and to steer their understanding and appreciation of these sights. Travellers could thus return to Britain laden with cultural knowledge – and often also laden with high-class souvenirs: paintings, sculptures, ceramic works, fragments of ruins, and other goods with which to adorn a home and demonstrate the good judgement of the purchaser.

This contact with Continental Europe had a significant influence upon patterns of taste within Britain and upon new cultural production. In architecture, painting, music, and other fields, imported styles were to be found alongside native forms and traditions. Sometimes these different styles merged or were conjoined – as, for example, when gothic buildings were given neoclassical interiors. At other times they became the basis for tension and conflict – as when William Hogarth, perhaps the best-known and most enjoyed illustrator of eighteenth-century life, objected to the popularity within the art market of continental Old Master styles, which appeared to him to be leaving little scope for the development of British painting. Overall it was a remarkably dynamic period for the arts – in terms of both the production of new works and the culture of discussion and argument surrounding them.

The growth of artistic production and consumption

'Our Sight is the most perfect and most delightful of all our Senses', wrote Addison in 1712, in the first of several *Spectator* essays addressing what he called the 'Pleasures of the Imagination' – pleasures 'such as arise from visible Objects, either when we have them actually in our view, or when we call up their Ideas into our Minds by Paintings, Statues, Descriptions, or any the like Occasion' (Bond 1965, III, 535–7). Promoting an idea of ocular epicureanism, Addison was writing when there were already many wonders to please the eye, and throughout the century the sense of sight was further appealed to as architects, gardeners, painters, sculptors and other artists and artisans were employed in the enrichment of Britain's visual environment.

It was certainly a boom time for architects and builders. When William III came to power, London was still being rebuilt after the Great Fire of 1666 – a disaster which had opened up many new architectural opportunities, particularly for Sir Christopher Wren (1632–1723), who worked on designs for some 52 new churches for the capital, among them St Paul's Cathedral, completed in 1711. After the revolution, Wren continued to gain commissions for major building projects: for example, the Royal Hospital at Chelsea and Greenwich Hospital – both homes for retired servicemen. As new civic buildings went up, domestic architecture was also changing the layout and look of London, as wealthy aristocrats and businessmen aspired to have impressive city homes. It was at this time that many of the grand squares and streets of Westminster were laid out and constructed – with building lines and vistas carefully planned to please the eye. In fact, with a growing population, and with an increasing proportion of that population living in towns and cities, it was a period of significant urban reconstruction and expansion throughout Britain. In the countryside, there were also many opportunities for architects, as landowners – both established and *nouveau riche* – invested in lavish estates and built new country houses, or, more commonly, remodelled and extended existing ones. In the 1750s, for example, work began at Osterley Park in Middlesex to transform the main building from a Tudor mansion into a neoclassical palace; similarly Wimpole Hall in Cambridgeshire had its seventeenth-century origins masked behind a neoclassical façade.

The investments made in the restyling of old houses demonstrate how very significant matters of taste had become. These architectural makeovers usually involved some practical improvements, but fashion typically came before function. And when new buildings were designed for affluent clientele, matters of style and ornament were high priorities. The architectural mode of choice for many was Palladianism – a style derived from the buildings of ancient Rome and filtered through the designs and writings of the Italian architect, Andrea Palladio (1508–80). Baroque styles, offering exuberant grandeur with bold, massy forms and rich colouring, were widely used in the early part of the period – not least by Wren who, through his own innovations, was central in the development of an 'English Baroque' movement. But Baroque's popularity was being eroded by the 1720s as the lighter classicism of Palladianism was increasingly favoured, not least because of its promotion by Richard Boyle, the third Earl of Burlington (1695–1753), an amateur architect and avid sponsor of the arts. Later in the period, the refined neoclassical designs of the Adam brothers, Robert (1728–92) and James (1732–94), became the zenith of good taste, while throughout the century an alternative to classicism was offered by gothic styles, which were derived from buildings from the middle ages. A gothic folly was enough medievalism for many, while some enthusiasts wishing to stand aside from the classicist mainstream commissioned whole gothic houses, complete with towers, turrets and castellations.

The rash of building projects generated, of course, a growing demand for the skills of other artists and craftsmen working within the business of visual pleasure. Designers and decorators of interiors thrived – Robert Adam, in fact, was admired more for his work on the interior proportions of rooms, and on details such as fireplaces, pilasters and mouldings, than for his designs for whole buildings. High-class cabinet-makers, such as Thomas Chippendale (1718–79), supplied suitably elegant furniture for the houses of the rich, and through pattern books, such as Chippendale's *The Gentleman and Cabinet-Maker's Director* (1754), the styles developed by elite designers were disseminated and made available for emulation and imitation. There were widely differing kinds of furniture to choose from; Chippendale, for example, was not dogmatically attached to any single style, as his pattern book shows, with its offering of a 'Large Collection of the Most Elegant and Useful Designs of Houshold Furniture in the Gothic, Chinese and Modern Taste' (1754, titlepage). On a smaller scale, there was a vibrant market for ornate glassware, silverware, and particularly ceramics, production of which was starting to become more industrialized. Josiah Wedgwood (1730–95) opened his Staffordshire pottery works in 1759, and by means of a number of technical innovations was able to begin larger-scale production of high-quality ceramics. Such developments allowed the pleasures of the imagination to be experienced by greater numbers, as people from the middling orders increasingly became able to buy a little piece of upper-class life.

Around the country houses of the rich, gardens and estates provided another area for indulgence in visual pleasure and for experimentation with different aesthetic approaches to nature. In landscaping the estates of the upper classes, there was typically a need to balance function with design: there was still a concern with producing saleable timber, for example, and most country houses would have a substantial kitchen garden, but large swathes of land were remodelled purely to increase the satisfaction given by pleasing views, interesting walkways and relaxing arbours. Following the designs of eminent landscape gardeners such as William Kent (1685–1748) and Lancelot 'Capability' Brown (1716–83), artificial lakes and streams were created, temples and other follies were erected, hillocks and valleys were reshaped, and copses were felled and new trees planted – it was a labour-intensive and expensive business.

It was at this time that the idea of the informal 'English garden' – *le jardin anglais* – became fashionable. In contrast to more formal approaches to garden design which had earlier been popular in Britain and remained so on the Continent, the 'English garden' involved a paradoxical aesthetic in which the goal of cultivation was a landscape which appeared natural. And adding to the paradox, the ideas of nature involved were in large part derived from art – from landscape painting, and especially that of Claude Lorrain (1600–82) and Nicolas Poussin (1594–1665), French artists who had spent most of their careers in Italy and who posthumously gained many British admirers due to their works being encountered on the Grand Tour. Claude and Poussin provided images for imitation of gently picturesque landscapes, while designers wishing to introduce more threatening, craggy features within a landscape could turn for inspiration to the work of another painter, the Italian Salvator Rosa (1615–73), who was also widely admired in Britain.

Painting, quite aside from its role in shaping the landscape, was, of course, a rich source of visual pleasure in itself – and it was one which came to be enjoyed by a public far larger than the elite groups given the run of upper-class mansions and gardens. With regard to landscape painting, continental artists were generally the most celebrated in Britain – it was a high compliment for the landscapist Richard Wilson (1714–82) to be called the 'English Claude' – and more broadly, in fact, the British art scene was permeated with foreign influences. Continental Old Masters from the Renaissance and seventeenth century commanded great respect – with painted copies and engravings allowing many who could not see the originals to become acquainted with the works – while Britain's prosperity attracted living painters and engravers from all over Europe. The German Sir Godfrey Kneller (1646–1723), who gained the position of 'Principal Painter' to William and Mary, was just one of the more prominent émigré artists who thrived among Britons willing to invest in the arts. At the same time, though, there were many native achievements in paint, with some British artists, such as Joshua Reynolds (1723–92), paying great homage to aesthetic ideals derived from continental forebears, while others, particularly William Hogarth, attempted to forge a school of painting that was not in thrall to these influences – that was shaped less by academic rules than by the close observation of modern British life.

In painting, as with other art forms, architecture was a driving force behind growing demand. To add to the grandeur or elegance of buildings, painters were frequently employed to provide ceiling and wall decorations. The inner dome of St Paul's Cathedral, for example, was adorned with religious images by Sir James Thornhill (1675–1734), a highly respected painter who also created works for Wimpole Hall and other private and civic buildings. For Greenwich Hospital, Thornhill produced one of the most remarkable paintings of the period: an enormous ceiling painting commemorating the achievements of the Glorious Revolution – patrons of the arts were often keen to exploit the potential of paint to convey a political message. New buildings also created a demand for movable paintings on canvas, and while many thousands of works were being imported from Europe, buyers were also acquiring paintings produced in Britain, or were commissioning works for specific settings or of particular subjects.

There was plenty of work for portraitists. Kneller produced numerous acclaimed portraits – his subjects including many of the literary figures of his day – and it was common for members of the elite classes to have themselves or family members painted or to commission so-called 'conversation pieces' depicting several members of a family together in a single scene. Reynolds and Thomas Gainsborough (1727–88) both prospered, turning out portraits of the wealthy. Hogarth also produced portraits and conversation pieces, but he never became established as a 'society painter' in the manner of Reynolds and Gainsborough. Hogarth, in fact, carved out a rather unique position within British art as a documenter of contemporary society, a satirist, and a visual storyteller. Indeed, the narrative element in Hogarth's work is so strong that he is sometimes accorded a type of 'honorary writer' status – his work is included within literary anthologies, for example, and is often seen to have more in common with the novels of, say, Henry Fielding than with the productions of his contemporaries working within the visual arts. This is in part because of the wide social range of his subject matter. He was as interested in representing low life as high life; he produced sensitive portraits of servants, for example, and many of his narrative works depict humble characters and stories of the poor.

Hogarth's democratic way of seeing marked him out from many of his contemporaries, but he shared with other artists – including Reynolds and others who followed aesthetic ideals quite contrary to Hogarth's – a commitment to expanding the *public interest* in the visual arts. Hogarth's devotion to engraving was one way of making art accessible to a wider reach of society: having begun his career as an engraver, he treated many of his paintings not as unique objects but as components within a larger cultural enterprise involving the production and selling of prints. His best-known narrative works – *A Harlot's Progress* (1732), *The Rake's Progress* (1735), *Industry and Idleness* (1747) and *Marriage à-la-Mode* – gained their popularity not from the original oils, but from their publication as black-and-white prints. Hogarth, though, was also keen to explore new ways of getting people to look at paintings.

With his career beginning in the 1720s, Hogarth was working for most of his life before the idea of the public art exhibition had been established; pictures would be displayed in auction houses, and sometimes in coffeehouses prior to being sold, but there were no public galleries as such. Hogarth contributed to their emergence by seeking out new exhibition spaces: this was a way of steering clear of the established commercial market which, with its respect for old and foreign notions of good painting, was not the best environment for the kind of work he wished to see promoted. In the 1730s, for example, he arranged for works by British painters, particularly Francis Hayman (1708–76), to be displayed at Vauxhall Pleasure Gardens. This venue was a type of amusement park – one of several in London – which offered a range of genteel entertainments, as well as refreshments and opportunities to mingle, converse and flirt whilst strolling through the ornate gardens. Vauxhall was the most popular of London's pleasure gardens – the entrance fee was smaller than at the more upmarket Ranelagh Gardens at Chelsea – and with large crowds gathered there in search of new entertainment, it was an ideal location for getting pictures seen. Later, in 1746, Hogarth arranged for London's Foundling Hospital to be used as an exhibition space for British artists – a venture which was applauded by both artists and visitors – and from the mid-century further exhibition venues were opened to the public.

Reynolds was involved in the most important of these: the galleries of the Royal Academy of Arts. The academy was founded in 1768, with Reynolds as the first president, and thousands of visitors were attracted to its London exhibitions, initially staged in rooms in Pall Mall and, after 1780, in plush new surroundings at Somerset House. Lofty ideas of connoisseurship lay behind the establishment of the academy: Reynolds, who would present an annual discourse on art, and other early members were seeking to create an institution from which ideas of high art – the ideas that informed their own artistic production – could be disseminated among the viewing public and could shape public taste. In the process they were, of course, increasing the status and commercial value of their own works within the market, but not everyone attending the exhibitions was a potential buyer. The Royal Academy's exhibitions had an influence upon the market, but they also attracted a new type of viewer and played an important role in creating something tangential to the market: a *public* for art – a large body of people interested in looking at paintings, discussing paintings, and displaying discernment in their judgements.

The growth of a culturally concerned public involved other art forms too – not least the theatre and music. Musical performances were a standard part of the repertoire of entertainment on offer at the theatres (about which more will be said in the next chapter), but in itself music was becoming an increasingly significant part of British cultural life, both in London and in the provinces. As with the visual arts, foreign influences were strong. Italian opera, for example, became extremely fashionable following its introduction to the London musical scene early in the century, and numerous foreign musicians and composers were attracted to London. George Frederick Handel (1685–1759) spent much of his life in England, where he achieved a long string of successes, beginning with *Rinaldo* (1711), the first Italian opera written specifically for the London stage. Italian castrati singers were greatly admired in Britain – for example, 'Farinelli', the stage name of Carlo Broschi (1705–82), became a star attraction in London, as the city began to be counted among the most important centres on the European musical circuit.

The father of Wolfgang Amadeus Mozart (1756–91) made a point of visiting England when he was touring Europe with his prodigiously talented son, and they stayed for over a year, from 1764 to 1765, providing entertainment for numerous audiences at court, in the houses of the aristocracy, in public halls, as well as in a public tavern. Music could be heard in Britain's churches and cathedrals; outdoor orchestras entertained visitors to the pleasure gardens; and as new exhibition rooms were found for painting, so new assembly rooms and concert halls opened to cater for the increasingly large public audiences interested in attending musical performances. For example, the Pantheon, an elegant venue in Oxford Street, opened in 1771, with a central rotunda which, at the time, was one of the largest rooms in Britain. Shortly afterwards the Hanover Square Rooms were opened with a seating capacity of more than nine hundred. And music spread beyond these venues too, as it was made available for performance by amateurs through such publications as *The Songster's Magazine; Being a Choice Collection of the Newest Songs Sung at Ranelaugh and*

Vauxhall Gardents, the Theatres Royal, and all other Places of Public Entertainment (c. 1785).

There was a proliferation of these 'Places of Public Entertainment' during the eighteenth century. Being entertained and engaging in cultural life was becoming a goal for an increasingly large proportion of the population, and there was a constant supply of novelty to keep audiences and viewers interested. Throughout the period British culture was continually enriched by an influx of influences and artists from abroad and through the creative exertions of Britons themselves.

2

Literature in the Eighteenth Century

Introduction
Major Genres
Literary Groups

INTRODUCTION

This chapter provides an introduction to eighteenth-century literature, primarily through discussions of different types of writing: firstly, the periodical essay, a form which truly flourished in the period, and thereafter poetry, drama and prose fiction – the main genres into which imaginative literature is usually divided. The aim here is to outline the general contours of those genres, the ways in which they developed, and their positions and functions within eighteenth-century society. In conclusion there are short accounts of the period's major literary groups, the output of which was usually not restricted to a single genre.

Note that the use of the term 'literature' here is a modern one which would not have been recognized in the eighteenth century itself when 'literature' was generally used to refer to the world of scholarship. Samuel Johnson's *Dictionary*, for example, defines 'literature' as 'Learning; skill in letters'. At that time 'poetry' was sometimes applied in a broad sense to refer to plays and prose fiction as well as to poems, but the concept of 'literature' (or 'Literature') as a category embracing such works of imaginative writing had yet to be institutionalized as it is now.

Note also that this chapter focuses upon *new* literary productions, and so does not give a complete picture of the literature being published and read at the time which naturally included many older works. Classical literature was widely reprinted, both in the original Latin or Greek and in new translations as booksellers reached out to a wider market of readers, many of whom had not received the classical education that would allow them to read the originals. Religious works also thrived. The Bible was regularly reprinted in large numbers. In poorer households, if there was any book at all it was likely to be the Bible, while classic sermons were also popular. And the works of older British poets and playwrights – for example, John Milton (1608–74), Ben Jonson (1572–1637), and, most of all, William Shakespeare (1564–1616) – were widely reprinted. When considering the contexts of eighteenth-century literature, it is important to consider such literary precursors as well as contemporary publications and events. There was, though, undeniably a massive production of new material as well as a *diversification* of the literary genres and subgenres in the marketplace. The old and the new rubbed shoulders, as the blueprints inherited through literary traditions were emulated but also reworked or rejected by authors operating in a changing and expanding literary culture which offered great opportunities for experiment.

MAJOR GENRES

Periodicals and periodical essays

Many eighteenth-century authors cut their teeth by writing contributions for periodicals – that is, short, regularly published journals or magazines, often printed on just a single sheet of paper, which became increasingly common in Britain from the late seventeenth century. Periodicals were a crucial conduit for new writing; in themselves, they cannot be said to have comprised a genre for they presented short works of many different kinds – poems, anecdotes, book reviews, theatre reviews, fiction, parliamentary reports, and so on – but they became known particularly as an outlet for *essays*, a towering standard for which was set early in the period by Joseph Addison and Richard Steele (1672–1729), the collaborators behind the *Tatler* (1709–11) and the *Spectator* (1711–14). Addison's and Steele's essays addressed a wide range of topics, such as politics, trade, manners, philosophy and aesthetics, all with a general purpose of entertaining, enlightening and refining their readers. A main aim, as Addison put it in the *Spectator* (No. 10), was 'to enliven Morality with Wit, and to Temper wit with Morality' (Bond 1965, I, 44). A further goal was to shift plenty of copies. Steele, in particular, needed the income, but both authors were also keen that their writing should have real social impact – that their essays should become a talking-point and influence patterns of public behaviour and belief. This cultural penetration was achieved both through the regularity of the publications – the *Tatler* appeared thrice weekly, while the *Spectator* appeared daily between March 1711 and December 1712, and then was revived as a thrice-weekly paper for a run in 1714 – and through extremely wide circulation. Addison, reckoning that each copy of the *Spectator* would be passed around some twenty readers, suggested he reached around 60,000 people in the capital alone (Bond 1965, I, 44). He was probably exaggerating here in a bid to promote the *Spectator* as *the* essential reading for anyone wishing to be in tune with the affairs of the day, but both the *Tatler* and the *Spectator* were tremendously popular, and they remained so throughout the period when published in collected editions – the essays proved to be of enduring interest, much praised for their wit and stylistic elegance, despite the topicality of many of the matters they addressed.

These periodicals were important in part because they put printed matter at the heart of social exchange and public debate. As Addison was keen to note, periodicals were often *shared* – they became closely associated with the chocolate and coffeehouses of London, where they could be handed around from customer to customer and could feed into the general conversation such establishments fostered. Indeed the register of many periodicals derives from such sociable settings: many *Tatler* essays are presented as written in 'White's Chocolate-house', while the *Spectator* appears as a type of journal recording the goings on and correspondence of 'Mr. Spectator's Club', a motley assemblage of contemporary character types. The printed matter, then, poses as an extension of the clublike world in which its consumption is assumed to take place, and this enhanced the ability of periodicals to trigger and lead debates. Steele, for example, was able to use a *Tatler* essay (No. 25) to invite reflection on the ethics of duelling – a barbarous practice, in Steele's eyes, quite inappropriate for the modern civilized society which he and Addison were engaged in forging and refining through their writing. And the characters of the *Spectator* could be used to explore social tensions and to shape – or attempt to shape – readers' political views: the inclusion, for instance, of Sir Roger de Coverley, an old Tory squire, and Sir Andrew Freeport, a representative of new money derived from trade, allowed Addison and Steele to dramatize the shifting contours of society as well as to promote their own Whig politics by generally speaking up for the trading interest.

While the general market for periodicals flourished throughout the century, individual journals were often short-lived, sometimes running to just a handful of issues or lasting just a few weeks or months. Many foundered because they failed to attract readers, but several very successful periodicals were unsustainable for long since they were the work of just a few hands, or sometimes of a single author who might be drawn away towards other projects. Samuel Johnson wrote all but five numbers of the *Rambler* which appeared twice weekly from March 1750 until March 1752. Later he wrote weekly *Idler* essays, which appeared as part of the *Universal Chronicle, or Weekly Gazette*, and again he achieved a two-year run, from April 1758 to April 1760.

But as some periodicals ceased, many others sprung up – around the mid-century, London readers could usually choose from some thirty different periodicals on the market. Some periodicals appealed to particular interests with specialized themes – the theatre, for example, or medicine – while others offered broader content. One of the most enduring was the *Gentleman's Magazine*, established in 1731 by Edward Cave (1691–1754), who collected and edited contributions from a team of writers to produce a substantial 'general interest' monthly for men. This was one of the first periodicals to have a real impact in the provinces as well as in the capital. While relying on his regular contributors, Cave was an effective recycler of already published material: with copyright legislation still in its infancy, the legality of reprinting a text in a summarized, abridged, rephrased or translated form was uncertain, and the *Gentleman's Magazine* was by no means the only periodical to garner cheap copy through such processes. Cave was also open to receiving unsolicited material – as were other editors – and this gave many would-be writers the opportunity to try their hand at authorship. One of the first published works by the novelist Laurence Sterne, for example, was a poem published in the *Gentleman's Magazine* in 1743.

In fact, with a constant demand for material, the periodical press brought many authors their first taste of publication, and could provide a modest income for industrious individuals seeking to establish themselves in the book trade. This was how Johnson survived his first years as an author, working for Cave and others, while Oliver Goldsmith began his erratic literary career with a meagre living from hack work for periodicals after having arrived penniless in London in 1756. Writers for periodicals were predominantly male, but women were not excluded – indeed several periodicals targeted specifically at women helped to establish an idea of women readers as a particular, distinct sector of the literary market, and this in turn created openings for women's authorship and editorial work. In July 1709, in response to Addison and Steele's work, the *Female Tatler* was established under the editorship of Delarivière Manley (1663–1724). With a good deal of scandalous content this journal lasted under Manley for some four months, and then was revamped by others to survive as a more respectable publication until March 1710. Addison and Steele were echoed again later in the *Female Spectator* (1744–46), a monthly publication established by Eliza Haywood, and there were other periodicals, such as the *Lady's Magazine, or Entertaining Companion for the Fair Sex* (1770–1837), which were pitched specifically at women readers and which often drew upon the resources of women writers.

Periodicals, then, played an important role within society through their energizing and shaping of public discourse, while within the business of literary production they were crucial to the proliferation of *professional* authors – something of a new species in the eighteenth century, which evolved so as to supply the quantities of suitable new material sucked up within a growing market for printed matter. Periodicals were also, as I have suggested, closely connected to other genres. Often written or edited by authors also producing plays, poems and fiction, they themselves regularly included poetic and fictional content. They were also the main outlet for literary *reviewing* – a further phenomenon which grew as more and more works poured out from the presses and as readers began to seek guidance through the deluge of new literature, the vast diversity of which I hope will become apparent in what follows.

Poetry

The cultural importance of poetry

For readers of the twenty-first century faced with an eighteenth-century poem it is worth while taking a mental leap and imagining a time when poetry really *mattered*. Poetry, of course, still matters today, but as modern poets will admit – often with frustration – poetry has become the poor relation of literary genres, enjoying nothing like the prevalence or the public importance which the writing and reading of verse once had. In the eighteenth century the use of poetry was commonplace. With its metrical arrangement and with other formal particularities, poetry involved manipulations of language which marked it out as an exceptional mode of expression when compared with standard prose, but in terms of its applications poetry was a far more normal aspect of daily life than it is today. We can elaborate upon its status in the period with some more pointed generalizations:

- There were a great many outlets for verse which brought a wide sector of society into contact with poetry. In the theatres, plays were frequently written in verse, while prose drama was typically framed by a verse prologue and epilogue (playwrights were commonly referred to as poets). Essays were often prefaced by a snippet of verse. Newspapers and periodical magazines would regularly publish poems. Novels sometimes included passages of verse, while a further outlet was found in popular ballads and songs. In addition, sales of printed volumes of poetry were increasing – not only the works of individual poets, but also poetic compilations or 'miscellanies'.

- The range of the subject matter addressed in verse was extremely wide, and topics were often approached in quite commonplace ways. Since the Romantic period, poetry has tended to be seen as an introspective, lyric mode of writing best suited to the expression of personal reflections and deeply felt responses to the world. In the eighteenth century, however, poetry was treated as a more public form of expression appropriate to all manner of everyday topics such as politics, money, gardening, manners, cookery, married life, theology, the weather, fishing, philosophy, how to make cider, the topography of London, ice houses, drinking, scientific innovation, laundry, and so on. Individual experience and feeling was certainly addressed in verse, but poetry was typically turned more towards the social than the personal. Events of major public importance were addressed in poems – for example, *Windsor Forest* (1713) by Alexander Pope is in part a Tory celebration of the Treaty of Utrecht which brought the War of the Spanish Succession to a close – and poems could invigorate public discourse concerning such events.

- While a number of poems dealing with topical matters were finely wrought and have an artistry which has allowed them to endure as aesthetic achievements (*Windsor Forest* is again a case in point), there was a lively market for more casual 'occasional' poetry – verse which was not agonized over and written to last, but produced simply to comment on a recent event for the benefit of contemporaries (Johnson used the phrase 'temporary poems' for such verse when defining 'Grubstreet' in his *Dictionary*).

• Poetry was often used for extended developments of arguments and debates – in fact, some eighteenth-century poems are structured as dialogues or conversations through which a debate about a particular issue is articulated. Or sometimes a poem would elicit a poetic response from another writer so that together they formed a debate or conversation in verse. For example, when Stephen Duck (1705?–56) wrote of the strains of being an agricultural worker in 'The Thresher's Labour' (1730), a forceful riposte was offered by Mary Collier who paraded the equal or greater hardships of domestic service in 'The Woman's Labour' (1739). Numerous poems of the period take the form of verse epistles or letters, where a particular addressee is imagined and engaged in a type of conversation. The discursive tendency explains the great length of many works: the period's long works are typically epic in terms of argumentative scope rather than story, and reading them demands an alertness to their development as chains of ideas and opinions.

• Unlike in previous eras, a number of writers were able to earn their livings from poetry – poetry became a *profession*. Early in the period, large-scale translations of classical poets were particularly lucrative: John Dryden (1631–1700) – the first official poet laureate – made a fortune with his translations of Virgil (1697), and later Pope established himself through sales of his translation of Homer's *Iliad* (1715–20), the success of which led him subsequently to tackle the *Odyssey* (1725–26). Original poetry could also bring substantial rewards. Pope increased his wealth with profits from his original works, while Duck was able to leave his life as a thresher behind, due not only to sales of his works but also to royal patronage (alongside the developing market economy of print, patrons continued to play an important role). At the same time, many professional poets struggled to sustain themselves – the distressed, hungry poet was a recognized type long before the famous demise of Thomas Chatterton (1752–70) – and poetry remained a semi-professional or amateur pursuit for many who wrote poetry as a sideline to other careers or as a form of creative leisure.

Such generalizations as these need to be treated with caution, for they do not tell the whole story of a vastly varied period of poetic production, and it is easy to point out examples which do not fit in with this overall picture. The type of introspection associated with Romanticism, for example, can be found very early in the period – for instance, in the work of Anne Finch (1661–1720) – and Romanticism, of course, by no means closed the door on poetic treatments of a wide range of topics beyond the personal and subjective. Furthermore, while the publication of verse increased, poetry had a base which was even broader than the expanding print market, for there remained an active culture in which poetry was circulated privately in manuscript form, particularly among aristocrats, who were rarely interested in profiting financially from print, and who sometimes regarded publication as a form of debasement to the standards of the common marketplace. Lady Mary Wortley Montagu, for example, wrote primarily for an exclusive group of upper-class friends (although a number of her poems were pirated and published).

With such reservations, though, it is worth while recognizing that the prevailing conception of poetry was different in the period. Poetry was not seen as a specialist, minority interest, indulged within the confines of exclusive coteries; it was a significant and normal part of public life and social interaction, and the nature of many poems – in terms of subject matter, rhetorical stance, and range of reference – was determined by that cultural position.

The social reach of poetry

Poetry was written and read by large numbers from right across the social spectrum. Many poets emerged from the labouring classes despite the generally low levels of education and literacy within that sector – indeed, slight education could sometimes be an advantage as ideas of untaught genius and 'natural' poetic expression became increasingly celebrated among readers and patrons from higher ranks. Duck and Collier, together with the milkwoman-turned-poetess Anne Yearsley (1756–1806) and Mary Leapor (1722–46), a kitchen maid, have become well-known examples of such low-born poets, but there were many more whose works are still being rediscovered – a recent anthology *Eighteenth-Century English Labouring-Class Poets* (2003), stretching to three large volumes, showcases the great extent and range of poetic activity within this class. Poetry was also open to both women and men, although for a woman seeking acceptance and respect as a poet there were often obstacles to be overcome. In the Restoration, John Wilmot, the Earl of Rochester (1647–80), had written aggressively that 'Whore is scarce a more reproachfull name, / Then [*sic*] Poetesse' (Rochester 1984, 83); thereafter women writers would still sometimes be confronted with hostility if they ventured to publish their work and with condescending assumptions about the extent of their possible talents. 'Alas! a woman that attempts the pen, / Such an intruder on the rights of men', wrote Anne Finch in 'The Introduction', a manuscript poem which vividly expresses the difficulties facing female poets:

> Did I, my lines intend for publick view,
> How many censures, wou'd their faults persue, . . .
> They tell us, we mistake our sex and way;
> Good breeding, fassion, dancing, dressing, play
> Are the accomplishments we shou'd desire;
> To write, or read, or think, or to enquire
> Wou'd cloud our beauty, and exaust our time
>   (Winchilsea 1974, 4–5)

Nonetheless, as with the writing of fiction and drama, poetry did become an increasingly respectable female pursuit and there was a marked increase in the publication of poetry by women. In 1712, Richard Steele, faced with naming, in an essay in the Spectator (No. 314), 'the chief Qualification of a good Poet' was ready with a simple answer: 'To be a very well-bred Man' (Bond 1965, III, 138). The decades that followed showed Steele to be quite wrong, as men and women with very different types of breeding were to prove their poetic skills.

Poetry also had a wide geographical reach. London was the centre for poetic production, but many provincial poets rose to prominence – for example, the Newcastle-born Mark Akenside (1721–70) and Anna Seward (1742–1809), the so-called 'Swan of Lichfield'. Scotland produced several of the period's leading poets. Some Scots embraced the union of 1707 and entered into the poetic culture of England and the new Britain – for example, James Thomson (1700–48), who moved south and authored not only one of the period's most widely read poems, *The Seasons* (1730), but also the patriotic 'Rule Britannia' (1740). For other Scots, the union and there-after the failure of the 1745 Jacobite rebellion were rather spurs to protect local cultural traditions, and beginning with Allan Ramsay (1686–1758) there arose a movement to revive vernacular Scots writing and to re-explore folk traditions so as to bolster the idea of Scottishness within Britain. Late in the period, Robert Burns (1759–96), albeit an admirer of many English poets, was a major contributor to this movement with his *Poems, Chiefly in the Scottish Dialect* (1786). Involving a more distant and more romantic gaze into the past, there was also, from the mid-century, a widespread taste for poetic antiquar-ianism, and here again the peripheral regions of Britain were crucial. 'Primitive' poems, often giving accounts of the early history of Britain, were unearthed and refashioned for con-temporary readers by poets and poet/editors such as Thomas Percy (1729–1811), who was responsible for an influential col-lection of *Reliques of Ancient English Poetry* (1765), and Thomas Gray (1716–71), who, following extensive research into British literary history, adopted the voice of a thirteenth-century Welsh poet in *The Bard* (1757). Such projects typically involved a good deal of invention. The most renowned and celebrated 'ancient' poems of the period, *The Works of Ossian* (1765), purported to be translations from the Gaelic of a third-century Highland bard, but as a craze for Ossian flourished it emerged that the texts were largely the result of embellishment and invention on the part of their 'translator', James Macpherson (1736–96). Wales had a similarly creative antiquarian in 'Iolo Morganwg' – the bardic name adopted by the more prosaically entitled Edward Williams (1747–1826), a forger of texts supposedly conveying ancient druidic traditions. Such poetic antiquarianism was not entirely a turn away from the contemporary – indeed, since many of these poems are concerned with the ancient history of Britain, they could offer indirect reflections on the modern issues of national identity which the recent union of Britain had ignited.

The changing canon of eighteenth-century poetry

Eighteenth-century poetic culture, then, was nourished by a remarkably diverse range of voices. And it is a diversity which, for modern readers, continues to increase as the works of long unheard poets are reprinted or published online, adding to a wealth of 'new' poetic material from the period which, from the 1980s, started to become widely available due to a number of significant anthologies. Two collections in particular – *The New Oxford Book of Eighteenth-Century Verse* (1984) and *Eighteenth-Century Women Poets* (1989), both edited by Roger Lonsdale – brought many forgotten poets to light again, and in the process they challenged existing notions of an eighteenth-century poetic canon comprised of a procession of big names (almost entirely male) from Dryden to the early Romantics. Such a canon now seems exclusive and reductive, and as eighteenth-century poetry has become a wider and more variegated field, the idea of a grand narrative within which the period's verse can comfortably be emplotted has become problematized. Traditionally the period has been seen in terms of basically three phases:

- An early phase of neoclassicism and satire, during which ancient Greek and Latin poetry was widely translated and imitated, and classical forms were adopted and adapted for modern purposes – particularly by urban satirists (notably Dryden, Pope, Swift and Gay who flourished in the combative political climate of the reigns of William and Mary and Anne and of the subsequent Walpolean era.

- A mid-century age of sentiment (sometimes dubbed 'pre-Romantic'), which saw a decline of satire, a growth of regional poetry and of interests in native forms, and an increasing emphasis upon feeling and explorations of melancholy, as in the works of 'graveyard' poets such as Robert Blair (1699–1746), Edward Young (1683–1765), and Thomas Gray in his celebrated 'Elegy Written in a Country Churchyard' (1751). The mid-century is also associated with powerful religious meditations in verse.
- An era of poetic and political revolution – with the work of William Blake (1757–1827), whose *Songs of Innocence* (1789) comes right at the end of our period, and, moving onwards, with the 'proper' Romanticism of William Wordsworth (1770–1850) and Samuel Taylor Coleridge (1772–1834).

A ghost of this narrative remains a part of modern understandings of the trajectory of eighteenth-century verse – it is hard to deny, for example, that the early eighteenth century was an era of outstanding satirical verse – but as the chorus of poetic voices has grown the story has become more intricately threaded and complicated, and we are reminded that there are always counter energies at work.

But it is not only shifts in the canon which have altered approaches to eighteenth-century poetry – so too have changing critical attitudes, not least towards the nature of the period's neoclassical tendencies and its fostering of poetic invention and innovation. Influential critics have sometimes denounced much of the period's verse as uninspired and hamstrung by classical precedents. The poet and critic Matthew Arnold (1822–88), for example, famously declared in an essay of 1888 that Dryden and Pope were 'not classics of our poetry, they are classics of our prose' (Arnold 1970, 359). It is an odd remark (as well as a patently untrue one), but what Arnold seems to be suggesting here is that, along-side these poets' discursiveness and argumentativeness (qual-ities usually associated with prose), there is in their works a lack of true 'poetry' – of 'poetic' inventiveness and original-ity – when compared with, say, the playful conceits created by the metaphysical poets of the Renaissance and the Romantics' supposedly inspired expressions of poetic genius. For Arnold, Dryden and Pope were 'masters of the art of ver-sification' (Arnold 1970, 359) but not true poets – well-trained journeymen rather than *inspirés*. But there is a good deal more poetic creativity and inventiveness in eighteenth-century poetry than Arnold's remark might suggest.

Poetic forms: traditions and innovations

Classical poetry was certainly greatly admired at the time – hence the demand and marketability of translations of the classics – and many poets regarded emulation of classical forms as an essential component of true poetic achieve-ment. 'Before the Basis of the Frame you lay, / The famous Plans of *Greece* and *Rome* survey', urged Richard Blackmore (1654–1729) in a 1706 verse essay, *Advice to the Poets* (Womersley 1997, 185). Popular classical models included the pastoral and the related eclogue, with their idealizations of rural life, as well as the georgic, which, deriving from Virgil's *Georgics*, involved a more realistic attention to aspects of the rural and allowed for the blending of informative accounts of agricultural and manufacturing processes with political and philosophical reflection. This form was widely adapted for application to the modern world – notably in *Cyder* (1708), an influential work by John Philips (1676–1709), *The Fleece* (1757) by John Dyer (1699–1757), and *The Sugar-Cane* (1764), a georgic set on the Caribbean island St Kitts, then a British colony, by James Grainger (1721?–66). Horace and Ovid provided models for the verse epistle – the prime vehicle for the period's 'conver-sational' poetry – while Pindar came to be widely emulated, particularly from the mid-century, as writers explored the lyrical possibilities of the ode, a form traditionally applied to the expression of lofty emotions.

Epic poetry was much discussed in the period's criticism and literary theory but it was not a form that many poets tackled in practice. Pope and others were more at home with the mock-epic – the form of Pope's celebrated *The Rape of the Lock* (1712–14) and *The Dunciad* (1728–43) – in which the grandiose conventions of epic are applied, with a satirical inappropriateness, to trivial and everyday matters. For poets writing about contemporary Britain, particularly with the type of 'warts and all' approach favoured by Pope and Swift, a serious epic mode would have been quite unfitting, but much could be achieved by inverting the form. Mock-epic could ironically highlight a *dearth* of noble or heroic qualities in contemporary life – as when Pope produces a tongue-in-cheek heroic depiction of the poet laureate Colley Cibber (1671–1757) as the supreme dunce within a culture teeming with dunces. But epic's elevation of its objects to a grand scale also allowed for less condemnatory explorations of the everyday. Working with the epic convention of extended description allowed poets to probe what would usually be regarded as trivial – the nature of a teapot, for example – and in the process suggest that such aspects of life are actually *worthy* of careful poetic examination. As well as epic, other classical forms were also creatively overturned or redirected towards a modern topic. London's high society took the place of pastoral Arcadia in a series of 'Town Eclogues' (1716) by Wortley Montagu, and the city was in focus again in Gay's 'urban georgic', *Trivia; or, the Art of Walking the Streets of London* (1716). The classics were revered, but were nonetheless treated very loosely and inventively when they served as inspiration for new writing.

It is worth noting here that the most widely used poetic genres of the period had considerable formal elasticity, particularly with regard to their overall length. More rigid poetic forms were sometimes employed: the sonnet, for example, with its fixed structure of fourteen pentameter lines, was used to great success by several poets – Gray and Thomas Warton (1728–90), for example, and later Charlotte Smith (1749–1806), author of a series of *Elegiac Sonnets* (1784).

Indeed, there was something of a 'sonnet revival' from the mid-century after a long period of neglect. In general, though, poets favoured more flexible forms which were suitable for lengthy, wide-ranging explorations of a topic. Where the author of a sonnet must compress ideas and must carefully discipline language so as to fulfil the demands of the form, the author of, say, a georgic has greater scope to develop ideas, to explore their ramifications, to build expansive patterns of imagery, to debate and to digress – in short, to keep adding more lines until the topic has been examined to the poet's satisfaction. Like the sonneteer, the writer of a georgic is, of course, still concerned with disciplining language – with forging phrases that function within a metrical scheme – but without a fixed endpoint there is less obligation to compress. Indeed, it was not uncommon for poets to go back to works which had already been published so as to revise them and, usually, to add to them. This is why many poems of the period can be found in different versions and are presented as having several years of publication or a range of years rather than with a single date. Pope's *The Rape of the Lock*, for example, was first published in 1712 as a poem of two cantos (the Italian for 'song', a 'canto' is a traditional subdivision of an epic or narrative poem). Pope continued to work on the poem and an expanded five-canto version appeared in 1714, and following this he added further lines for its republication in *The Works of Mr. Alexander Pope* (1717). Later in his career, Pope undertook even more elaborate processes of revision and expansion with *The Dunciad*, published in different versions in 1728, 1729, 1742 and 1743. This poem is a mammoth work of satire which ridicules a parade of literary rivals and other prominent contemporaries, and as Pope worked on his new versions he was in part *updating* the work – modernizing its satirical targets so as to refresh the work's relevance to contemporary readers. Many other poems of the period were, at some point, both published and 'in process' – brought to a state of completion, yet at the same time malleable and unfinished, and laden with potential for *renewed* dialogue with eighteenth-century readers.

This flexibility was possible not only because of the overall openness of the genres but also because of the type of poetic building-blocks which writers tended to favour. The eighteenth century is well known as a great age for the couplet, and particularly heroic couplets – that is, rhyming pairs of pentameter lines with a predominantly iambic rhythm, such as these from the beginning of Pope's *Epistle to Burlington* (1731–44):

> 'Tis strange, the miser should his cares employ,
> To gain those riches he can ne'er enjoy.
> Is it less strange, the prodigal should waste
> His wealth, to purchase what he ne'er can taste?
> (Pope 2006, 243)

Poets mostly used end-stopped, 'closed' couplets; meaning would often be allowed to run across the line ending *within* a couplet, as happens between the third and fourth lines above, but there is usually a stop or break of some kind at the conclusion of the second line. Structured in this way, the couplet proved to be an eminently serviceable poetic unit. When treated individually it was well suited to containing succinct, epigrammatic observations – as in the lines above (particularly the opening pair) – since its boundaries fostered a concision which could lead to pithy, witty expression. But couplets could also be readily strung together to create larger poetic structures, and a sequence of couplets could quite easily be 'opened up' as new ideas came to the poet during composition or if new material was to be inserted later on. Joined together, couplets served as an effective vehicle for narrative and they could propel an argument or chain of thought forward since their simple rhyme scheme tends to maintain a sense of onward progression – unlike many broader patterns of rhyme which, when spanning several lines, can have the effect of flipping the reading experience back on itself. And many different rhetorical effects could be achieved through heroic couplets. As pentameters, the lines have sufficient length to uphold a ponderous, stately pace, or a melancholic languor, as in, for example, Wortley Montagu's 'Verses on Self-Murder' (1736):

> With toilsome steps I pass thro' life's dull road,
> No packhorse half so weary of his load;
>   (Fairer and Gerrard 1999, 191)

But internal breaks could also be introduced so as to create more lively rhythms and effects, as in the opening of Pope's *An Epistle to Dr Arbuthnot* (1735):

> 'Shut, shut the door, good John!', fatigued I said,
> 'Tie up the knocker, say I'm sick, I'm dead.'
>   (Pope 2006, 337)

Brisker rhythms could also be achieved through shorter lines, and tetrameter couplets (that is, rhyming pairs of lines with four feet) also proved to be a popular poetic vehicle – one much used by Swift.

Couplets did not appeal to all poets, though, and many writers pointedly rejected altogether what Milton, in his preface to *Paradise Lost* (1667), had famously condemned as 'the troublesome and modern bondage of rhyming' (Milton 1997, 55). Milton, in fact, was widely admired in the eighteenth century – lauded as a national literary hero who, with *Paradise Lost*, had provided England with its own great epic – and it was Milton's verse which was used to provide the model for long poetry's main alternative to heroic couplets: blank verse. Like heroic couplets, blank verse – that is, sequences of unrhymed iambic pentameters – was well suited both to narrative and to the building up of discussions and arguments, and it came to be widely used, not least by patriotic writers who, like Milton, saw it as a peculiarly *native* mode: with its absence of rhyme – commonly presented as a *freedom* from rhyme – it could readily be associated with ideas of British liberty. Philips' *Cyder* did much to popularize Miltonic blank verse, and indeed Philips was widely seen as Milton's successor – in Thomson's *The Seasons*, for example, Philips is hailed as the second poet (after

Milton) 'Who nobly durst, in Rhyme-unfetter'd Verse, / With British Freedom sing the British Song' (Thomson 1981, 169). *The Seasons* itself became a celebrated feat of blank-verse composition which further advanced the cultural status of the Miltonic form, and other prominent poets, such as Edward Young and William Cowper (1731–1800), would come to write extensive works in this mode.

Another popular verse form with strong native credentials was the ballad. Where Miltonic blank verse maintained a status as a 'high' form, ballads were ranked lower down the cultural hierarchy, but they were nonetheless enjoyed by readers of all classes, and while associated with traditional oral culture they regularly appeared in print and were popularized through anthologies such as *A Collection of Old Ballads* (1723), Percy's *Reliques of Ancient English Poetry*, and *Old Ballads, Historical and Narrative, with Some of the Modern Date* (1777). Indeed, ballads provided ground for the collision of ideas of 'high' and 'low'. Addison was an early advocate of the form, sharing with the polite readers of the *Spectator* (No. 70) his relish for 'the Songs and Fables that are come from Father to Son, and are most in vogue among the common People' (Bond 1965, I, 297). For Addison and many later readers, the appeal of ballads was located in their simplicity – in their 'inherent Perfection of Simplicity of Thought' which could at once be 'the Delight of the common People' and 'appear beautiful to the most refined' (Bond 1965, I, 297–8). To those refined readers, a ballad offered an opportunity to be emotionally moved, together with a confirmation of personal sophistication through recognition of the lowness of the form. In the *Spectator* (No. 85), for example, Addison found 'a despicable Simplicity in the Verse' of the popular ballad tale of 'Two Children in the Wood', yet he insisted that 'because the Sentiments appear genuine and unaffected, they are able to move the Mind of the most polite Reader with inward Meltings of Humanity and Compassion' (Bond 1965, I, 362).

Sanctioned for consumption by the tasteful, for whom the anthologies provided convenient selections, ballads still remained a staple within popular culture – not least since when produced as single-sheet 'broadside' publications they were among the cheapest forms of entertainment available. And while associated with the past, the ballad form was not only a relic: it was regularly exploited for telling stories of the modern world or commenting upon events and people in the news. Proliferating at election times, ballads were used for celebrating or condemning politicians, and they were often harnessed for popular protest – against taxation, for example, as in the 'The Congress of Excise-Asses, Or, Sir B--ue S--ng's Overthrow: A New Ballad' of 1733:

> But, Britons, take Care,
> Of Excises beware,
> For if you once let in this Dragon,
> With his Teeth and his Talons,
> And Crew of Rabscallions,
> He'll not leave you're A---s a Rag on.
>   (Anon., 1733, 8)

This is not exactly the type of ballad that Addison had in mind for the tickling of polite sensibilities, but such writing was nonetheless an important part of the varied fabric of eighteenth-century poetic culture. Expression in verse – 'high' and 'low', refined and crude, shaped by the classics or otherwise – was integral to the everyday life of the nation.

Drama

The changing world of the theatre

For a visitor to London's Covent Garden theatre on Monday 30 May 1759 – an unexceptional day – the first performance on the bill was Shakespeare's *Hamlet*. Then after this main piece there was a two-act farce by Samuel Foote (1720–77) entitled *The Englishman Return'd from Paris* – a satire poking fun at contemporary manners and at the French which had proved popular since its first performance in 1755. Then there were dances – a comic piece called 'The Drunken Peasant' and the recently choreographed 'The Milkmaid's

Holiday' – as well as two songs: 'A Favourite Ballad, call'd The Goldfinch's Address to Chloe' and 'The Country Wedding'. And interspersing these performances were spoken prologues and epilogues. It was a fairly typical line-up of entertainment for the time: a mixed programme offering intense tragedy, light comedy, music, a bit of pastoral sentimentality and some visual clowning – what might now be separated into 'high' and 'low' culture were presented side by side. The next day the dances were performed again, while the main piece had been replaced with *King Henry IV, Part One* and there was a different afterpiece too. Such was the milieu of varied, rapidly changing entertainment for which new dramatic works were written in the eighteenth century. Theatre managers had clearly come under pressure to provide a broad range of entertainment with something to appeal to everyone, whether in the pit, box or gallery.

Over the course of our period, in fact, British theatre culture changed in a number of important respects, many of which had an impact upon dramatic writing:

- The theatres developed from the elite, court-centred insti-tutions they had been after their reopening at the Restoration in 1660 and became more socially heteroge-neous. Members of the middling and lower orders started to attend the theatre in significant numbers – for one thing, admission became more affordable – and this came to be reflected in new plays addressing the concerns of these classes.
- Theatres became more respectable institutions, shedding some, but not all, of their reputation for immorality and debauchery.
- As the theatres became generally more middle class, more explicitly moralistic dramas came to be written and per-formed.
- Theatres became bigger, with new buildings constructed to accommodate larger audiences, and existing buildings extended.
- The division between the audience and performers became

more marked: the proscenium arch became a standard
feature in new theatres, and whereas early in the period
some audience members had been seated directly around
or even on the stage, they became more separated. Greater
spectatorial distance opened up the possibility for more
orderly performances with fewer interruptions from audience members seeing themselves as part of the dramatic
event. Rowdiness did, though, remain a feature of theatrical culture – Karl Phillip Moritz, a Prussian visitor to
London in 1782, observed the audience in the cheap upper
gallery causing the 'noise and uproar, for which the English
play-houses are so famous' (Moritz 1795, 72) – and there
were incidents of rioting throughout the century.
- Scenery and lighting became more sophisticated, and
  were often used to create elaborate naturalistic effects.
- Predominant acting styles changed with grand declama-
  tory techniques being challenged, particularly from the
  1740s, by more naturalistic styles.
- Plays became popular as printed works so that 'theatrical
  culture' spread beyond the theatres themselves.

Plays: new trends in the new century
Many of these changes were set in motion during the decade
following the 1688 revolution – a time when there arose widespread criticism of the theatres as dangerous centres of vice
with repertoires dominated by bawdy drama which seemingly
legitimized depraved behaviour. Most prominent among
hostile commentators was the Reverend Jeremy Collier
(1650–1726) whose *A Short View of the Immorality and Profaneness
of the English Stage* (1698) encouraged a heated public debate
concerning the proper social function of the theatre. William
Congreve (1670–1729) was one of the playwrights Collier
targeted. Congreve had found great success in the 1690s
writing complex comedies of intrigue with witty, fast-paced
dialogue – particularly *The Old Batchelor* (1693) and *Love for
Love* (1695) – as well as a tragedy, *The Mourning Bride* (1697).
For Collier, Congreve's comedies were insupportable foun-
tainheads of vice and blasphemy – 'almost all the Characters

in the *Old Batchelor*', he complained, 'are foul and nauseous' (Collier 1974, 4) – and such views attracted many supporters as Collier brought into focus a growing public dissatisfaction with licentious theatrical culturè. Controversy endured well into the new century, being fuelled by numerous printed works such as William Law's *Absolute Unlawfulness of the Stage-Entertainment Fully Demonstrated* (1726), a vehement Christian attack upon the stage which would be reprinted throughout the period. Some critics sought to ban theatrical entertainment outright, while others, including Collier, aimed rather to *reform* the stage – to harness its social potential to a more instructive and improving purpose. The stage, they argued, could serve a function akin to that of the Church – the opportunity of a large public gathering could be exploited for the dispersal of proper values and models of good conduct. The essential point of a play, for Collier, was 'to recommend Vertue, and discountenance Vice' (Collier 1974, 1).

Collier's campaign was publicly opposed by leading dramatists including Congreve, Dryden and John Vanbrugh (1664–1726), but new dramatic writing showed that within the theatre world there was support for a redirection of dramatic entertainment. Congreve's *The Way of the World* (1700), now regarded as his masterpiece, was not a success when it first appeared, and Congreve did not write in the Restoration comic mode again. A more successful dramatist at the beginning of the new century was George Farquhar (*c.* 1677–1707) whose innovations in his plays have led to him often being seen as a transitional figure between Restoration and eighteenth-century dramatic trends. In a 'Discourse upon Comedy' (1702), Farquhar himself wrote of comic drama as 'an agreeable Vehicle for Counsel or Reproof' and a means 'of schooling Mankind into better Manners' (Farquhar 1988, II, 377–8), and his plays do show a didactic edge when compared with many comedies from the preceding decades. From his debut with *Love and a Bottle* (1698), Farquhar centred his plays on a classic staple of earlier comedy – the rake – but they typically develop to show the taming of libertinism as the rake is reformed through the influence of a woman. Farquhar's *The*

Constant Couple (1700) was a major success – with the rakish Sir Harry Wildair it offered some of the mischievous attractions of earlier comedy, while the ultimate honour of the character and the conclusion of the play in marriage provided satisfaction for the more morally inclined among the audience.

Farquhar was also influential in shifting the focus of drama away from the metropolitan *beau monde*. In his two most enduring plays – *The Recruiting Officer* (1706) and *The Beaux' Stratagem* (1707) – Farquhar set his action in the provinces, in Shrewsbury and Lichfield, and he gave provincial characters a dignity which had been largely reserved to urban characters in seventeenth-century comedies. Indeed, in earlier plays, such as William Wycherley's *The Country Wife* (1675), the countryside had often been portrayed as a backward region of dullards, innocents and fools – a trope providing dramatic and comic contrast to the sophistication of the city. Further innovation was found in Farquhar's work in his giving lower-class and impecunious characters central positions in his plots. *The Beaux' Stratagem* revolves around gentlemen of broken fortunes, highwaymen and an innkeeper – the play's huge success showing that there was an audience for contemporary drama dealing with reaches of society outside the world of the fashionable elite.

At the same time, there was a strong public demand for tragedy, which was satisfied with new dramas by, among others, Nicholas Rowe (1674–1718), an admirer and emulator of Shakespeare, who produced one of the several eighteenth-century editions of Shakespeare's works. Among theorists and practitioners of drama in Britain there were neoclassicists who maintained that proper tragedies should uphold the Aristotelian unities of time, action and place. John Dennis (1657–1734) and Thomas Rymer (1641–1713), for example, were vociferous upholders of neoclassical dramatic theory in critical writings, while Peter Motteux (1660–1718) was observant of it in his *Beauty in Distress* (1698). Rowe approached tragedy with a freer hand – the example of Shakespeare justified his approach, and audiences were clearly approving of a liberal attitude to dramatic rules, even if some critics were not.

Rowe's verse tragedy, *Tamerlane* (1702), became standard fare in repertoires, but it was his so-called 'she tragedies' – works depicting the downfall of a heroine – for which Rowe became best known. Rowe's *The Fair Penitent* (1703), again written in verse, is, as the prologue put it, a 'melancholy Tale of private Woes' showing 'Men and Women as they are', and audiences were enthralled by its depiction of an abandoned heroine who ultimately commits suicide (Rowe 1756, I, 230–1). The female suffering in his *The Tragedy of Jane Shore* (1714) likewise caught the sympathies of the public.

Among other tragedians was Joseph Addison who struck a popular chord with *Cato* (1713), a classical tragedy in verse which retells the story of the Stoic Cato's defence of Rome against the tyranny of Julius Caesar. Staged when the issue of the monarch's role and succession were still central within British political discourse – the death of Queen Anne was imminent – it is a good example of how drama could be used for articulating indirect political commentary. When Cato's sorrow over the death of his son is outweighed by his grief for the loss of liberty in Rome, the public could readily draw connections with what could conceivably happen in Britain, and Addison had clearly anticipated that Cato's declaration 'O Liberty! O Virtue! O my Country!' would prove rousing for Whigs within the audience – the line, apparently, was often met with cheering (Addison 1713, 53).

Whig sympathies were also appealed to in the works of Susannah Centlivre (*c.* 1667–1723), a prolific and popular author who experimented with several genres but found her greatest success with comedies. The theatre, throughout the period, offered opportunities to many women writers, including Mary Pix (1666–1709), Delarivière Manley, Eliza Haywood, Frances Sheridan (1724–66), Frances Brooke (1724–89), Elizabeth Griffith (1727–93), Hannah Cowley (1743–1809), Hannah More (1745–1833) and Elizabeth Inchbald (1753–1821), all of whom, like Aphra Behn before them, cultivated writing for the stage alongside other literary projects. Indeed, as with most male playwrights, dramatic authorship was rarely a professional specialism but was

biography of Congreve, 'Comedy grew more modest, and Collier lived to see the reward of his labour in the reformation of the theatre' (Johnson 1905, II, 223). But that is not to say that the theatre became a sanctimonious and prudish institution – there are no truly neat lines of development in theatre history, and a narrative of progressive chastening does not capture all the strands of eighteenth-century theatrical culture. Lewd comedies by writers such as William Wycherley (1641–1716) and George Etherege (*c.* 1634–92) continued to be performed, while in newly authored plays, which would often revolve around love, desire, courtship, and the arrangement of marriages, the display of sexuality remained one of the functions of performers, particularly actresses who would provide audiences with erotic spectacle, not least when playing 'breeches parts': female actresses would sometimes play male roles, as well as female roles which involved male disguise. As Steele himself observed in the *Spectator* (No. 51), 'When a Poet flags in writing Lusciously, a pretty Girl can move Lasciviously, and have the same good Consequence for the Author' (Bond 1965, I, 217).

One development which can be fairly stated is that, following Farquhar, drama continued to become more broadly based in terms of the class origins of the characters represented on the stage. In *The Conscious Lovers*, Steele articulated the concerns of the merchant classes very explicitly, including bold assertions of their new significance: 'we Merchants', one character insists, 'are a Species of Gentry, that have grown into the World this last Century, and are as honourable, and almost as useful, as you landed Folks, that have always thought your selves so much above us' (Steele 1723, 62–3). Later *The London Merchant* (1731), a tragedy by George Lillo (1693–1739), explored the plight of a low-born hero as he is led into a life of crime, and ultimately to penitence and execution. Like Steele's play, *The London Merchant* also speaks for the merchant classes – underlining their essential role in society – and it spawned further tragedies set in middle- or lower-class environments (often these are called 'domestic tragedies' or 'bourgeois tragedies').

The criminal underworld was showcased in a very different kind of play by John Gay. *The Beggar's Opera* (1728) was an extremely successful and generically innovative 'ballad opera', in which Gay blended dramatic dialogue and music, setting new words to traditional folk and ballad tunes. It is a satirical work and a principal purpose of the 'low' setting was to demonstrate, as is observed in the play itself, 'a similitude of Manners in high and low Life', and to suggest that criminality bubbled beneath the polite veneer of elite society and more or less held sway within political circles (Gay 1728, 57). It was clearly aimed at the government of Walpole, suggesting that Walpole himself was no better than the leader of a gang of thieves. In fact, the theatre at this time regularly served as a platform for satire, much of it aimed at Walpole and his government. Henry Fielding gained popular success with a number of burlesques – works parodying and satirizing 'high' dramatic forms like heroic tragedy – as well as anti-government satires. In *Pasquin, A Dramatic Satire on the Times* (1736) and *The Historical Register for the Year 1736* (1737) – works self-consciously addressing the here and now of British life – Fielding portrayed corruption within election practices and launched pointed attacks against members of Walpole's government. In 1737, the government responded to its critics by passing a Licensing Act – the most significant piece of theatrical legislation of the period.

The Licensing Act and mid-century drama

The Licensing Act imposed a monopoly on the London theatres, limiting their number to three: Drury Lane, Covent Garden, and the Haymarket Opera House. The Act furthermore required all new plays to be submitted to the office of the Lord Chamberlain for approval prior to performance – they could be approved for performance, or approved so long as certain cuts or changes were made, or they could be turned down outright. The Licensing Act undoubtedly put a damper on dramatic writing. Fielding, for example, had written 25 plays in the eight years leading up to the Act, but he turned away from the newly censored world of the theatre and chose to redirect his creative energies into prose fiction. Nonetheless new drama continued to be written, much of it by actors and theatre managers. David Garrick (1717–79), who following his stage debut in 1741 became the star performer of the mid-century, was not only highly influential as an actor and manager, but he also wrote original plays and afterpieces and adapted numerous existing works. George Colman (1732–94) combined dramatic authorship with theatre management, while the Irish actor Charles Macklin (1699–1797) made a name for himself as a playwright, shuttling back and forth between the London and Dublin theatre communities both to act and to arrange performances of his plays.

Macklin's career, in fact, provides a useful reminder that while London was undoubtedly the hub of British dramatic creativity, theatres were also thriving outside the English capital, most notably in Dublin, but also in the English provinces and later in Edinburgh. Indeed provincial theatre was indirectly given a boost when the Licensing Act limited the proliferation of theatres in the capital. Many of the larger provincial towns and cities, such as Bristol, York and Ipswich, had theatres early on, and an increasing number were opened and legitimized with royal patents in the latter half of the century. There were theatres in Norwich, Hull, Liverpool, Manchester, Newcastle, Brighton, Richmond and other towns, and they were often able to attract star performers particularly in the summer months when the London theatre season – roughly September to May – was over. In fashionable Bath – a Mecca of polite entertainment – the theatre gained an increasingly high reputation, becoming one of the major attractions; it was granted a royal patent in 1768 and leading London actors were keen to perform there. But it was Dublin which cultivated the greatest body of new dramatic writing outside London, even though many Irish dramatists found it necessary to migrate and break into the London scene in order to make a living. This was the route that the Irish Farquhar had taken and many followed him, including Macklin, Oliver Goldsmith,

Arthur Murphy (1727–1805), Hugh Kelly (1739–77) and later John O'Keeffe (1747–1833), a prolific writer of comedies and comic operas. Richard Brinsley Sheridan (1751–1816) was also of Irish extraction, and his father, Thomas Sheridan (1719–88), had begun his career in the Dublin theatre before moving to England.

While many Irish playwrights were able to succeed in London, representations of the Irish on the English stage were largely locked into an old 'stage Irish' stereotype. An Irish character was typically a 'Teague' – a foolish blunderer, often a fortune-hunter, and the butt of countless jokes. In fact, as the new nation of Britain developed, and as Britain became increasingly involved with the wider world through international trade and its empire, there was a proliferation of ethnic characters in newly written plays: we see the theatre functioning as a space for articulating and exploring the new ethnic relationships which were becoming significant in society at large. The colonial experience of Britons was also examined in plays such as *The West Indian* (1771) by Richard Cumberland (1732–1811) and Samuel Foote's *The Nabob* (1772), both of which address the experience of returned colonialists. Stereotyping remained strong, but some plays display a degree of resistance to stock modes of representation. In Macklin's *Love à la Mode* (1759), for example, an Irishman, a Jew, an Englishman and a Scot are pitted against one another in a campaign to woo a wealthy heiress – it is a courtship battle and ethnic contest in one. Macklin imbued his Irish character with qualities which mark him out from the conventional stage Irishman – he is neither a fool nor a fortune-hunter – and it is the Irishman who wins the hand of the heroine. In the process of empowering the Irishman, though, the play unreservedly deploys and re-enforces unflattering stereotypes of Jews and Scots.

With regard to genre, tragedy lost some of its popularity after the mid-century. In 1773 Goldsmith observed that for some years tragedy had been 'the reigning entertainment; but of late it has entirely given way to Comedy' (Goldsmith

1966, III, 209). But comedy was itself a wide and multifaceted category, and some comic works – so-called 'sentimental comedies' – were providing audiences with much of the emotional anguish more usually associated with the experience of tragedy. By this time the sanitization of the theatres had advanced further. Restoration comedies were being performed in new, cleaned-up versions or with cuts and revisions so as to satisfy, as one observer noted in 1780, 'the extreme delicacy of a refined age, whose ears are become exceedingly chaste' (Davies 1780, II, 331). Sentimental comedies, such as Hugh Kelly's *The False Delicacy* (1768) and Cumberland's *The Brothers* (1769) and *The West Indian*, appealed directly to these delicate audiences. Such plays have origins in earlier moral comedies like Steele's *Conscious Lovers*, and they usually involve middle-class characters being put through trials from which virtue emerges triumphant. Like the sentimental novels being written around the same time, they emphasize mankind's natural capacity for human benevolence and they include pathos-laden scenes inviting the response of tears.

Goldsmith dubbed such drama a 'species of Bastard Tragedy' in a provocative essay entitled 'A Comparison between Laughing and Sentimental Comedy' (1773), and together with Richard Brinsley Sheridan, he promoted the virtues of 'laughing comedy' in order to restore to the stage some of the humour found in the Restoration 'comedy of manners' mode (Goldsmith 1966, III, 212). Both writers met with great success – Goldsmith's *She Stoops to Conquer* (1773) and Sheridan's *The Rivals* (1775), *The School for Scandal* (1777) and *The Critic* (1779) were acclaimed in their day for their arresting characters, witty dialogue and ingenious plots, and they have since proved to be the most enduring post-Farquhar eighteenth-century plays. With such success, Goldsmith and Sheridan are often seen as great victors in this tussle of genres, not only due to the quality of their plays but also because of the persuasive and provocative ways in which they voiced their views – Goldsmith with his essay and Sheridan with a satirical portrayal of Cumberland as Sir Fretful Plagiary in *The Critic*. They did not, however, oust sentimental comedy.

The theatres welcomed the works of Goldsmith and Sheridan into repertoires which remained very varied and generically diverse, and which still had room for writers such as Cumberland.

It should be remembered that those repertoires also retained throughout the period many older works. For most people at the time, Britain's most important and respected dramatist was Shakespeare – indeed this was the period when Shakespeare became truly established as the 'national poet'. His plays were performed more than those of any other playwright, often in adapted and softened versions (the tragedy of *King Lear*, for example, was performed with a happy ending), and new printed editions of his works were produced throughout the century. Shakespeare became an idolized national figure – he was celebrated in verse and prose and in paintings and sculptures, and when Garrick arranged an elaborate Shakespeare Jubilee in Stratford-upon-Avon in 1769 it was clear that a culture of 'bardolatry' had truly arrived. It became acknowledged that Shakespeare was *nonpareil*, but audiences were still eager for new works which, more directly than Shakespeare, could offer dramatic explorations of contemporary events and issues.

Prose fiction

More than 'the novel'

The eighteenth century is often seen as a great age for the novel – as the period which witnessed the 'birth' of the novel or, as the title of an extremely influential study from 1957 by Ian Watt put it, *The Rise of the Novel*. Since the publication of Watt's book, this generic 'rise' has proven to be one of the hottest topics for scholars and students of the period's literature, and the nature of this 'rise' is still a matter of ongoing debate. What are the essential characteristics of this upwardly mobile genre? What factors lay behind its elevation on the literary landscape? Were particular writers or works the main driving-force, or do we need to look into the sociological conditions of the time to explore the seedbed of a burgeoning genre? Did novelists 'invent' the novel or did practices of reading and criticism also contribute to the settling of the form's characteristics? Was the novel really born at this time or does it rather have earlier – even classical – origins?

On many aspects of the novel's story scholars have not reached a consensus, but most would tend to agree with a basic premise: that at the beginning of our period the *idea* of 'the novel' (what was being referred to if people used the term) was only loosely formulated, whereas towards the end of the century a more stable idea had crystallized behind the general usage of the term – and that idea had much in common with modern understandings of what a 'novel' is. Defining that modern notion is itself problematic and limiting, but so as to have a working definition here we might cautiously refer to the *Oxford English Dictionary* (*OED*), according to which a novel is 'a fictitious prose narrative or tale of considerable length (now usually one long enough to fill one or more volumes) in which characters and actions representative of the real life of past or present times are portrayed in a plot of more or less complexity'. Not only was such an idea of the novel undeveloped in the earlier part of the period, but the term itself had not yet become the predominant label for long prose fictions. It rather jostled among many other terms which, in the expanding market for print, authors and booksellers were attaching to narrative fiction: 'romance', 'tale', 'life', 'fortunes', 'adventures', 'memoirs', 'expedition', and very commonly 'history', as well as 'true history', 'secret history', and other formulations. So when, for example, Daniel Defoe was writing *Robinson Crusoe* (1719), *Moll Flanders* (1722) and other works which we now usually think of as 'novels', he and his contemporaries did not think of them as such – and Defoe would not have considered himself or been considered to be a nove*list*. He wrote of his works as 'histories', while his title pages advertised the excitement of his stories with such phrases as *The Life and Strange Surprizing Adventures of Robinson Crusoe* and *The Fortunes and Misfortunes of the Famous Moll Flanders*. For some commentators, the very length of Defoe's works would actually have ruled them out of the category of 'the novel', since for a long time novels were commonly seen to be relatively short works – in his *Dictionary* of 1755 Johnson defined a 'novel' as 'A small tale, generally of love' and he apparently saw no reason to update the definition when he revised the *Dictionary* for a 1773 edition. However, by the turn of the nineteenth century, when Jane Austen (1775–1817) and Walter Scott (1771–1832) were writing, the idea of the novel as we now know it had become more firmly established. Austen, for example, saw herself as a novelist, and wrote confidently of 'novels' and 'novelists' in the modern sense in *Northanger Abbey* – a work published in 1817 but written some twenty years earlier. And the consolidation of the idea can be further seen in enterprises such as a 50-volume collection of fiction published in 1810 and revealingly entitled *The British Novelists*.

The novel has arguably now become *the* dominant literary genre, and it is certainly fascinating to explore how this state of affairs came about and to examine eighteenth-century fiction as a 'prehistory' to the novel, in which the form as we know it was inchoate and evolving. But we should remember that eighteenth-century authors and readers were not themselves as preoccupied with the idea of the novel as later historians of the genre. While many prose writers were experimenting with new narrative forms, they were by no means consciously trying to invent the modern novel yet somehow falling short and only coming up with half-successful prototypes. This is why I have entitled this section 'Prose fiction' rather than 'The novel', in the belief that it is worth while keeping in mind that:

- There is more in the huge body of fiction written in the period than the scattered ingredients of the modern novel.
- Sometimes thinking outside the framework of the modern novel when we read eighteenth-century fiction can help to avoid a sense of disorientation when we encounter things that may seem to be unnovelistic in a modern sense.

Let us consider, for example, *Robinson Crusoe* (for many critics, a strong contender for the title of first modern novel) in which we find much that is in line with received notions of what constitutes a novel. The 'characters and actions', to refer back to the *OED*, can be seen to be representative of 'real life': Crusoe is a plausible character, and his adventures – including the central story of his shipwreck and survival on a desert island – are related in a realistic manner which allows readers to believe in the settings and in the events that take place. But many modern readers find Defoe's handling of plot unsettling, particularly towards the end of the work, which can seem to go on beyond where it should have stopped. When Defoe has got Crusoe off the island, he does not simply round the story off but adds more adventures, such as a long sequence in which Crusoe's companion Friday taunts and kills a bear. Why does Defoe let the story continue (or 'drag on', as some would say) rather than provide the sort of formal neatness which we might find in a modern novel? We can perhaps account for this by remembering that Defoe was not writing a novel, but was rather offering his readers a collection of '*Strange Surprizing Adventures*'. He was providing entertainment – filling up readers' leisure time by allowing them to experience vicariously the dangers and challenges which Crusoe and Friday face, and for those readers episodes such as that with the bear could serve as an added bonus. And this was something Defoe was well aware of as he quickly capitalized on the public taste for such tales with a sequel, *The Farther Adventures of Robinson Crusoe* (1719). Defoe was simply not operating with the conception of plot which has come to be seen as integral to the idea of the novel, and so the work could readily be extended. Many other works of prose fiction from the period similarly present characteristics which can seem unnovelistic.

Plausibility is commonly seen as an attribute of the novel – this is implicit in the *OED*'s emphasis on the form representing 'the real life of past or present times' – yet implausibility was readily accommodated in the prose works of some of the most renowned writers. In *Gulliver's Travels* (1726), for

example, Jonathan Swift adopts a convincing mode of narration to convey a story which from plausible beginnings rapidly
veers off into realms of unbelievable fantasy (although some
early readers were apparently taken in by it). The work –
depicting Gulliver's voyages to the miniature and giant lands
of Lilliput and Brobdingnag, as well as a floating island,
immortal humans, speaking horses, and many more fantastic
creations – tends to preclude the type of reading experience
which conventional novels offer. It invites different interpretive strategies by which the fantasy is not *fully* entered into but
rather consumed with half an eye on its artificiality as a
means of generating commentary on the real world. As a
satirist, Swift was less concerned with writing a plausible,
coherent story in which readers could imaginatively immerse
themselves, than with coming up with inventive and witty
mechanisms for exposing what he saw as the ills and absurdi-
ties of human life and society. Gulliver himself is hardly a
coherent character – he is not like a 'proper', psychologically
developed character in a 'proper' novel, being more of a
device which is manipulated as the narration goes on, according to Swift's needs as a satirist.

Samuel Johnson's *Rasselas* (1759) is a very different type
of work but it displays a similar lack of concern for plausibility and realism. Here philosophical speculations and
observations are prioritized over efforts to draw readers into
a truly coherent fictional world. *Rasselas* is a type of oriental fable and its story, in which an Abyssinian prince and his
entourage depart from their home in a fantastical 'Happy
Valley' in order to explore different modes of life, is really a
premise for an extended enquiry into the nature of earthly
happiness. Johnson's characters, like Gulliver, are far from
'rounded', and they often seem more like mouthpieces
articulating positions within philosophical dialogues than
truly imaginable people. *Rasselas* is an absorbing work – but
not by virtue of qualities we usually associate with the
novel.

In fact, *Rasselas* was one of numerous oriental tales published in the period, many of them inspired by the popular

Arabian Nights Entertainment, volumes of which began to be published in English from 1704, as well as other imported and translated works such as *The Thousand and One Days: Persian Tales* (1714), *Turkish Tales* (1708), *Chinese Tales* (1725), and *Mogul Tales; or, The Dreams of Men Awake* (1736) – 'British' fiction, then, was not purely home-grown but was responsive to influences from abroad. Addison was an early emulator of these models and wrote fiction set in the orient for the *Spectator*, while later more extensive works with fabulous eastern settings and characters appeared such as *Almoran and Hamet* (1761) by John Hawkesworth (*c.* 1715–73) and Frances Sheridan's *The History of Nourjahad* (1767). A 'novel-centred' approach to the fiction of the period can have the effect of sidelining such tales as these. Indeed oriental fiction has long been something of a forgotten subgenre, albeit that *Rasselas* has enjoyed ongoing respect due in part to the high status of Johnson himself, but collectively these works formed a notable part of what was being written and read for much of the period.

The rise of the 'familiar' and the plausible
The popularity of oriental tales provides a reminder of the enduring appeal of the fabulous in the eighteenth century, but within the variegated culture of fiction there *were* nonetheless efforts to forge a different kind of writing which was concerned with more ordinary, 'familiar' matters and which treated them without recourse to the improbabilities of fantasy – a realist form of writing which would come to be central to the idea of the novel. The new breed can be seen emerging partly through a process of authors and readers moving beyond or rejecting existing story-telling traditions – particularly that of the prose romance – which increasingly came to be deemed inadequate for treating the realities of contemporary life. William Congreve's *Incognita; or, Love and Duty Reconcil'd* (1692) – a work of fiction which is dubbed a 'novel' on its title-page – provides in its preface an early and lucid formulation of the developing distinction between romances and the new form:

> Romances are generally composed of the Constant Loves and invincible Courages of Hero's, Heroins, Kings and Queens, Mortals of the first Rank, and so forth; where lofty Language, miraculous Contingencies and impossible Performances, elevate and surprize the Reader into a giddy Delight . . . Novels are of a more familiar nature; Come near us, and represent to us Intrigues in practice, delight us with Accidents and odd *Events*, but not such as are wholly unusual or unpresidented, such which not being so distant from our Belief bring also the pleasure nearer us. (Congreve 1692, preface to the Reader)

Congreve points to two principal areas of contrast here. Firstly, romances and novels differ in terms of the sector of society they portray: while romances are concerned with an elite, novels, for Congreve, are of a 'more familiar nature'; they have a nearness to 'us' – a revealing term, by which Congreve appeals to his readers and puts himself and the matter of his chosen genre on a level with them. Secondly, there will be no miracles in a novel as there would be in a romance; there will be 'Accidents and odd *Events*' – so as to make a worthwhile story out of ordinary life – but these will fall within the bounds of what rational minds deem possible. Congreve accepts that gratifications are available from both kinds of writing, but he is clearly promoting the 'nearer' pleasures of the novel above the 'giddy Delights' of romance.

In practice, fiction did not always operate according to such clear-cut distinctions as Congreve draws. *Oroonoko; or, The Royal Slave* (1688) by Aphra Behn, for instance, presents an uneasy melange of romance conventions and novelistic innovations. In Behn's story, Oroonoko is an African prince who is tricked into slavery and transported to a plantation in Surinam, an English colony in South America, where, after attempting to organize a revolt, he is brutally executed. His wife Imoinda is likewise enslaved, and when pregnant is killed by Oroonoko himself – a drastic means of avoiding their child being born into slavery and her being left a vulnerable widow. Behn presents the work as 'A True History' and promotes the idea of its veracity through a first-person, eye-witness narrator who insists upon the story's distance from poetic fantasy:

> I do not pretend, in giving you the history of this royal slave, to entertain my reader with the adventures of a feigned hero, whose life and fortunes fancy may manage at the poet's pleasure; nor in relating the truth, design to adorn it with any accidents, but such as arrived in earnest to him. And it shall come simply into the world, recommended by its own proper merits, and natural intrigues; there being enough of reality to support it, and to render it diverting, without the addition of invention. (Behn 1992, 75)

Opening the work in this way Behn sets up clear realist expectations and as the story progresses they are at times fulfilled – for example, in several passages of documentary-like description of Surinam (which Behn may herself have visited). Yet *Oroonoko* seems unable to escape an inheritance from romance: it displays precisely the type of constant love, heroic courage, 'miraculous Contingencies' and so on that Congreve identifies in the form. The high-born Oroonoko has a quite staggering nobility and an unmovable commitment to virtue: he is able to 'do nothing that honour should not dictate' (Behn 1992, 114), while the killing of his wife is presented as a 'brave and just' act of necessity (Behn 1992, 135). He also has a physical prowess which seems to defy the normal limitations of the body – at his grisly execution, for example, he manages to smoke a pipe while his genitals, ears, nose and one arm are cut off. Imoinda is similarly virtuous and courageous: she faces her death with a 'noble resolution' and joy that 'she should die by so noble a hand' (Behn 1992, 135), and the love she shares with Oroonoko is of an idealized, romantic form – unquestionably constant and expressed through the language of the eyes. The plot too contains romance elements, such as a remarkable coincidence by which Oroonoko and Imoinda, who are split apart in Africa and transported separately, are brought together again by chance when they turn up at the same plantation.

Oroonoko, with its conflicting constituents, appears to bear witness to a generic struggle which has not been fully resolved; published right at the beginning of our period, it represents an early and perhaps uncertain step in the direction of the realist novel. Given the wide and multifarious nature of literary culture, it cannot be said that there was thereafter any neat rise of realism alongside an erosion of romance, but there are nonetheless signs that a movement against romance developed during the period, and by the mid-century it was well recognized that a new form of fiction had arrived which, as Johnson put it in an essay of 1750 in the *Rambler*,

> is . . . precluded from the machines and expedients of the heroic romance, and can neither employ giants to snatch away a lady from the nuptial rites, nor knights to bring her back from captivity; it can neither bewilder its personages in desarts, nor lodge them in imaginary castles. (Johnson 1969, III, 19)

The new fiction which, in Johnson's phrase, exhibited 'life in its true state' (Johnson 1969, III, 19), was still being defined through reference to what it was *not*. And this applied not only in critical discourse but also in fiction itself.

Shortly after Johnson's essay appeared, a significant intervention into the generic battleground was made in *The Female Quixote* (1752) by Charlotte Lennox (1717?–1804). In this popular work, as in *Oroonoko*, novelistic and romance conventions are found side by side, but rather than being thrown together in accidental tension, here they are self-consciously juxtaposed in a fictional conflict – the work knowingly intervenes in contemporary discussions of fictional genres and their values. As its title suggests, Lennox's work is a spin-off from *Don Quixote* (1605–15), Miguel de Cervantes' celebrated story of a gentleman who becomes deranged by reading medieval and Renaissance romances and, being unable properly to distinguish fiction and reality, proceeds to view the world through the filter of romance and to model his conduct on the chivalric codes he has absorbed through reading. Comically dramatizing the incompatibility of romance ideals and reality, *Don Quixote* depends for its effects upon a recognition of two different fictional registers – that of the romances in which Don Quixote loses himself, and that of what Cervantes presents as the real world. It was a formula which proved extremely successful in eighteenth-century Britain – another sign of British fiction's enmeshment within a broader international literary culture – and as well as being available in a number of translations, *Don Quixote* was frequently imitated. Henry Fielding's *Joseph Andrews* (1742) did much to secure Cervantes' standing in Britain – its title-page proudly acknowledging its indebtedness to 'the Manner of Cervantes' – and there were a number of full-blown quixotic imitations which remodelled Don Quixote's knight errantry within a contemporary British context: *The Life and Adventures of Sir Launcelot Greaves* (1760–61) by Tobias Smollett (1721–71), *The Spiritual Quixote; or, The Summer's Ramble of Mr. Geoffry Wildgoose* (1773) by Richard Graves (1715–1804), and others.

   In Lennox's feminized version of the form, the heroine, Arabella, develops her quixotism through consumption of a 'great Store of Romances' while isolated in a remote castle: 'Her Ideas, from the Manner of her Life, and the Objects around her, had taken a romantic Turn; and, supposing Romances were real Pictures of Life, from them she drew all her Notions and Expectations' (Lennox 1989, 7). This is the premise for a succession of comic scenes in which Arabella's sense of herself as a romance heroine leads to collisions between her behaviour and real-world codes and expectations. The humour generally falls upon Arabella herself in the accounts of her misguided social conduct, but since her reading has given her a sense of personal importance and power, those scenes can also serve to highlight the limited range of options usually available to a woman in polite society – eccentricity brings with it a certain liberation. However, the work as a whole ultimately suggests that romance is something which needs a *cure*, and it concludes with Arabella being brought to her senses by means of a

fitting treatment: a medicinal lecture on literature, administered by a clergyman who helps Arabella come to recognize
what fictionality actually is. Redeeming Arabella, the clergyman condemns the 'senseless Fictions' she has read, 'which
at once vitiate the Mind, and pervert the Understanding; and
which if they are at any Time read with Safety, owe their
Innocence only to their Absurdity' (Lennox 1989, 374).
Importantly, though, he does not condemn all fiction and
fictionality outright. 'Truth is not always injured by Fiction',
he argues; falsehood has value so long as it maintains a
'Resemblance to Truth' (Lennox 1989, 377–8). Through
such passages, and through the overall trajectory of
Arabella's story, *The Female Quixote* provides a vivid demonstration of the advancement of the new type of fiction: a
credible form of fiction, which, as Congreve put it, was
'not . . . so distant from our Belief'. A mode of writing which,
while not dealing with actual historical truths, creates a
resemblance to what falls within the realm of human possibility had, by Lennox's time, become firmly established on
the literary map.

The rise of fiction's moral respectability

I have dwelt on *The Female Quixote* at some length for it serves
as a useful index of eighteenth-century shifts in priorities and
tastes regarding ways in which prose fiction can relate to and
mediate the real world. But it also leads us onwards to further
important issues concerning which there was radical change
over the course of our period:

- The *respectability* of prose fiction
- The association between prose fiction and *moral instruction*.

For Arabella's saviour the truth value of fiction is important
because he sees it as connected to *the personal and social value
of reading fiction as an activity*: different forms of fiction are
regarded as having different potential consequences for the
health and virtue of the reader. We tend to live now with an
idea that almost any form of reading is basically a good thing

– reading generally has a high social status, and is usually seen as superior to, say, watching television or surfing the internet. It is important to recognize, though, that formerly – particularly before 1740 – reading fiction had a far less secure status. Various factors, involving both the reading matter being published and the readership to which it appealed, contributed to this dubious cultural position:

• As levels of literacy rose, fiction was increasingly becoming a form of *mass* entertainment. It is impossible to establish a truly accurate demographic profile of readers, but the available evidence suggests that, while the novel is often seen as a middle-class phenomenon, readership actually stretched far across the social ranks, and included men and women from the aristocracy to the lower orders.
• The increasing availability of prose fiction attracted new *types* of readers, and in fact fostered basic literacy among people who, without a formal education, might learn to read in order to gain access to the burgeoning form of entertainment. New fiction generally demanded a lower level of literacy and education than many other forms of writing – it is rarely tied up in classical references, for example, and its 'familiar' concerns are usually addressed in language which closely resembles that of everyday life.
• Fiction appealed particularly to the young, and many eighteenth-century works are seemingly pitched at readers embarking upon adult life, with stories of young protagonists negotiating their way into the world.

Responding to such factors, moral watchdogs became concerned about the effects of fiction and saw in its consumption a range of potential iniquities from time-wasting and the neglect of normal duties to the corruption of the mind through excessive imaginative indulgence. It was assumed that the behaviour and beliefs of readers could be strongly influenced by works of fiction. 'These books', Johnson wrote, 'are written chiefly to the young, the ignorant, and the idle, to whom they serve as lectures of conduct, and introductions into life. They are the entertainment of minds unfurnished with ideas, and therefore easily susceptible of impressions' (Johnson 1969, III, 21). Moralists were concerned, therefore, that *proper* lessons should be advanced through fiction.

But what if *improper* fiction should gain a hold within the marketplace? This was exactly what many believed to be happening in the early part of the period, since a number of authors had recognized the saleability of *scandal* and were successfully tempting readers with piquant 'secret histories' – titillation rather than education. One such author was Aphra Behn, who, just prior to the 1688 revolution, produced an influential series of erotic narratives entitled *Love Letters Between a Nobleman and his Sister* (1684–87). Behn wrote, for the most part, in order to earn her living, and this work certainly demonstrates her commercial shrewdness for it offers one of the enduring appeals of fiction by seeming to open up a hidden world and providing privileged access to what is normally concealed – in this case, private actions and feelings and the confidences shared between intimate correspondents. Posing as a collection of letters, this work is also an early demonstration of the effectiveness of epistolary narration – a technique which tends to foster a sense of intimacy with characters, as readers are allowed, as it were, to look over the shoulders of the character-narrators as they write their private letters and let loose their inner thoughts.

With these attractions, Behn's *Love Letters* proved immensely popular and the type of scandalous intrigue it offered became the fuel of many works of 'amatory fiction', as the form has been called, including such best-sellers as Delarivière Manley's *Secret Memoirs and Manners of several Persons of Quality, of both Sexes. From the New Altantis. An Island in the Mediterranean* (1709) and Eliza Haywood's *Love in Excess* (1719). Alongside erotic titillation, such works often also incorporated indirect social commentary and gossip. Manley's *New Atlantis*, for example, is a *roman à clef* – it is a bundle of loosely connected episodes featuring characters based on real-life individuals from contemporary aristocratic and political circles, and Manley took pains to present her work as a corrective satire on the behaviour of these figures. She urged readers to draw connections between her fiction and their shared reality, and in the process invited the erotic pleasures of the work to be thought of as secondary to the nobler purpose of correcting the vices of the times. But such rhetorical strategies were not sufficiently powerful to overcome an image of wantonness, and there developed a significant body of opposition to amatory fiction – and indeed to fiction in general. As one protester put it, most works on the market could give 'no great pleasure; for either they dealt so much in the *marvelous* and *improbable*, or were so unnaturally *inflaming* to the *passions*, and so full of *love* and *intrigue*, that most of them seemed calculated to *fire* the *imagination*, rather than to *inform* the *judgment*' (Richardson 1965, II, 454).

In fact, the above words were uttered not by a real reader but by a fictional character – the eponymous heroine of *Pamela; or, Virtue Rewarded* (1740–42), a work by Samuel Richardson which arguably did more than any other eighteenth-century publication to overturn the low moral status of prose fiction. This enormously popular work was a crucial catalyst in the development of a reading culture which prioritized the moral potential of fiction's consumption. *Pamela* – and later Richardson's *Clarissa* and *Sir Charles Grandison* (1753–54) – not only voiced direct criticism of the existing fiction but offered an alternative form of entertainment with narratives laying clear emphasis upon the benefits of principled Christian behaviour. The servant-girl heroine of *Pamela* is held up by Richardson as a model of unshakeable virtue, and her story – told mostly in her own voice through letters and a diary – charts her dogged resistance to the sexual advances of her predatory employer. Ultimately her pursuer is reformed by her virtuous example, and he and Pamela are married: the reward for her virtue is social elevation and material advancement. Like the fiction of Behn, Manley and Haywood, then, Richardson's work revolves around amatory matters, but the chastity of the heroine is preserved until marriage and the narrative is heavily glossed with explicit moral lessons. As Richardson put it in a preface to *Pamela*, his aim was to 'Divert *and* Entertain', but at the same time 'Instruct, *and* Improve *the Minds of the* Youth *of* both Sexes'. This was fiction designed pointedly '*to inculcate* Religion *and* Morality' (Richardson 2001, 3).

Pamela proved both popular and controversial. It was widely celebrated for its piety – being recommended, for example, from the pulpit of an admiring clergyman – but some readers smelt hypocrisy and condemned *Pamela* as a type of veiled pornography revolving around a duplicitous heroine whose interests lay in the price rather than the preservation of her virtue. Such a reading underlies Henry Fielding's parodic retelling of the story in *Shamela* (1741), the most famous of numerous interventions in what became an animated public debate between 'Pamelists' and 'Antipamelists'. The controversy surrounding *Pamela* highlighted the difficulty of advancing an unambiguous moral message through fiction – a medium which typically offers a greater number of interpretive *options* than are found in a straightforward didactic tract. At the same time, the debate showed how important fiction had become within public discourse, and many subsequent writers, such as Sarah Fielding (1710–68) and Frances Sheridan, aspired to follow Richardson's example and exploit this popular form of entertainment to explore moral dilemmas and recommend codes of conduct.

Furthermore Richardson's tendency to moralize through *sentiment* – through appeals to his readers' emotions – was also followed by his emulators, and after 1740 numerous examples of 'sentimental fiction' were published in Britain. Sarah Fielding's *The Adventures of David Simple* (1744–53), for instance, aims to move its readers with a pathos-laden narrative which, like *Pamela*, showcases the virtue of its main characters as they face the dangers of a wicked world. Such works highlight the 'sensibility' of their heroes and heroines – their capacity to *feel virtue* – and they assume and appeal to that same quality in readers. Emotiveness, in fact, became an increasingly valorized quality in literature. Weeping – or being seen to weep over fiction – became a means of asserting the respectability of consuming fiction, and in a number of sentimental works the exercise of pathos is apparently an end in itself. *The Man of Feeling* (1771) by Henry Mackenzie (1745–1831) is a famously lachrymose work, which is really more maudlin than didactic – its effects are akin to those of Richardson's fiction, but it is less pointedly moralistic.

Diversity and experimentation

The growing emphasis upon plausibility, the increasing tendency to treat 'familiar' matters, and the rise in moral respectability are among the most significant general trends concerning prose fiction in the eighteenth century. There were also, though, publications which do not fit in with those developments and which remind us that there were other currents within the diverse culture of fictional production. Despite the influence of Richardson, the 1740s saw the publication of a notorious pornographic fiction, *Fanny Hill; or, Memoirs of a Woman of Pleasure* (1748–49) by John Cleland (1709–89). Cleland's work was soon suppressed, but its publication and the circulation of pirate editions are evidence of some readers' taste for racy erotica – an aspect of literary culture which rarely entered public discourse concerning fiction. And this period of unromantic, plausible fictions not only supported the oriental tales mentioned earlier but also saw the emergence of a new type of implausible romance: the gothic novel, a subgenre traditionally seen to have been initiated by *The Castle of Otranto* (1764) by Horace Walpole (1717–97). With a medieval setting and a plot filled with supernatural occurrences, Walpole's work was both innovative and compelling and its popularity testifies to the resilience of readers' interest in romantic fantasy; the marketplace could clearly accommodate a far-fetched tale, despite the disparagement being cast upon romance by proponents of the new, 'familiar' fiction.

As prose writers appealed to different tastes and interests, many were also keenly experimental with the ways in which they set about telling their stories, and so there is also great *formal* diversity within the fiction of the period. When Fielding wrote in opposition to Richardson, for example, he

was not only expressing his objections to the moral programme of *Pamela* but was also staging a formal challenge to
Richardson's technique. Where Richardson allows his characters to speak for themselves through letters, Fielding's pre-
ferred narrative method involves an assertive narrator who is
not directly involved in the story but controls the telling and
passes comments on characters and events. Other writers,
notably Defoe, gave the responsibility for telling to a single
main character – the first-person narrative mode of works
such as *Robinson Crusoe* and *Moll Flanders* is derived more from
autobiography than from any fictional precursor.

Some writers were also interested in experimenting with the
physical appearance of books – exploiting the possibilities of
print technology to create new effects. Probably the most bla-
tantly experimental fiction of the period is *The Life and Opinions
of Tristram Shandy* (1759–67), a comic pseudo-autobiography
by Laurence Sterne. In this constantly digressive work, Sterne
employs several different interwoven time-schemes, and he
includes numerous playful typographical devices: a black
page, a marbled page, a blank page, a misplaced chapter,
wavy lines to illustrate the progression of the narrative, and
other gestures which disrupt the flow of the text. In *Tristram
Shandy* narrative innovations are presented with acute self-
consciousness. Other works of the period typically display
their formal novelty with less bravado, but with an expanding
market for fiction, and with few established rules or conventions for telling long stories, it was necessarily an era of experimentation and innovation.

LITERARY GROUPS

The Kit-Cat Club

Established in the 1690s, the Kit-Cat Club was an influential
group of writers and politicians which met regularly for eating,
drinking and conversation as well as for the promotion of the
arts and of Whig political objectives. Its largely aristocratic

membership included the Duke of Marlborough, Robert Walpole, William Congreve, John Vanbrugh, Joseph Addison and Richard Steele. While Addison and Steele would become renowned for their development of ideals of refined sociability and polite conversation in their essays in the *Spectator* and the *Tatler*, the club's private meetings tended to be quite riotous – with, for example, readings of pornographic verse to accompany the drinking. Jacob Tonson (1655–1736) was a prominent member and, as the most powerful bookseller of the period, was a key mediator between the club and the wider world of print – meetings of the club came to be held in Tonson's house. It is possible that an early clandestine version of the club existed prior to the Glorious Revolution to promote the Whig cause. The club's name derives from Christopher Cat, a pie-maker and proprietor of a London tavern at which the first meetings were held.

The Scriblerus Club

The Scriblerus Club was established in 1713 and was a group of influential writers and politicians with shared interests in satirizing 'false taste' and modern learning. Its leading members were Alexander Pope, Jonathan Swift, John Gay, Thomas Parnell (1679–1718), Dr John Arbuthnot (1667–1735), physician to Queen Anne, and Robert Harley (1661–1724), who led the Tory ministry with the support of Queen Anne from 1710 to 1714. As an actual club, its existence was fleeting, as the members dispersed after the queen's death in 1714. However, the *idea* of 'Scriblerianism' had an influential afterlife since many of the personal connections endured and the literary aims of the club were followed up in later writings such as Swift's *Gulliver's Travels* and Pope's *Dunciad* – works which build elaborate fictional frameworks to contain satirical attacks on diverse aspects of modern society, particularly corruption in politics and the perceived baseness of modern cultural productions. In fact, some much later works, such as Sterne's *Tristram Shandy*, begun in the 1750s, are sometimes seen as 'Scriblerian', despite there being no personal association between the author and the club. The club's name (aside from the obvious connection with 'scribble') relates to a fictional character called Martinus Scriblerus. Collaboratively, the club's members produced *The Memoirs of Martinus Scriblerus*, a witty satirical fiction which was initially written piecemeal for private entertainment within the club but was published in 1741 as part of Pope's *Works*.

Bluestockings

The Bluestockings were a group of intellectual, literary-minded women who, from the mid-century, began meeting for the purposes of serious conversation. Men of letters were invited to attend the evening meetings, which pointedly challenged the idea that intellectualism should be a male pursuit and that women's conversation should revolve around trivial or domestic matters. Prominent among Bluestocking hostesses were Elizabeth Montagu (1720–1800) (dubbed 'Queen of the Blues' by Johnson), Elizabeth Carter, Hester Chapone (1727–1801), Mary Delaney (1700–88) and later Hannah More. The name apparently derived from the stockings of Benjamin Stillingfleet (1702–71), a learned invitee who, too poor to own evening dress, attended in his blue daywear. The mutual exchange within the group stimulated the members' production of a large and varied body of fiction, poetry, plays, translations, literary criticism and letters. In terms of literary production, then, the influence of the group does not really rest in any distinctly 'Bluestocking' work or works – it is difficult, for example, to point to a Bluestocking style or a single Bluestocking ideology which might be advanced through literature. The importance of the group lay more in its general promotion of women's intellectual powers which were exerted in various literary projects. The group is the subject matter, though, of Hannah More's 'The Bas Bleu; or Conversation' (1787), a verse commemoration of More's friends and of the culture of polite intellectualism they created.

Samuel Richardson's circle

The sensational publication of Richardson's *Pamela* in 1740 brought its author an enormous amount of public respect and recognition – on the Continent as well as in Britain – and with it came a power to influence literary culture which endured well beyond Richardson's death in 1761. Richardson was already well connected in the book trade prior to *Pamela*: he ran a successful London printing business and eventually rose to become Master of the Stationers' Company. With *Pamela*, he gained a wide circle of fans and disciples – many of them women, whose admiration he particularly enjoyed – and he worked to hold this community together through the exchange of frequent letters as much as through actual meetings. Letters – the vehicle of Richardson's fiction – were, then, also fundamental to his social life, and in fact his private correspondence had an impact upon his fiction, as he often sent his friends and acquaintances draft sections of his work and solicited their advice and criticism. Richardson was also encouraging of other writers who shared his interest in emotive, morally didactic fiction. He gave valuable support to, for example, Sarah Fielding, who, as well as producing her own fiction, addressed Richardson's second major work in *Remarks on Clarissa* (1749), one of the earliest works of criticism to focus on novelistic writing. Among others, Richardson also supported Charlotte Lennox, Frances Brooke, and Frances Sheridan, who dedicated her sentimental novel *Memoirs of Miss Sidney Bidulph* (1761) to Richardson as one in whom 'exemplary Goodness and distinguished Genius' were united – a fairly typical tribute to the pious master (Sheridan 1761, I, iii). Richardson's followers were rarely simple copyists: there is much more of interest in the works of, say, Lennox and Brooke than their literary debts, and there is great variety in the fiction written in Richardson's wake. But Richardson can nonetheless be seen as the driving-force of a significant mid-century novelistic movement and as a catalyst for a growth of didacticism in literature more generally.

Samuel Johnson's circle and 'The Club'

In the 1750s, Samuel Johnson, after a long struggle as a professional author, began to be recognized as a leading writer and intellectual – the highly respected creator of an extensive body of work including poetry, literary biography, periodical essays and his *Dictionary*. With a wide circle of personal friends and acquaintances within the book trade and within London's cultural milieu more generally, Johnson exerted considerable cultural influence both through his own example and through the assistance he offered fellow writers. For example, he famously saved Oliver Goldsmith from being arrested for debt by speedily arranging the sale of *The Vicar of Wakefield* (1766) to a bookseller – a typical move in which benevolence and an interest in nurturing literary culture were combined. Johnson's influence found a more formal forum in 'The Club' – later known as the 'Literary Club' – instigated in 1764 by Sir Joshua Reynolds, the portraitist who would become the first president of the Royal Academy of Arts. Meeting at a tavern in Soho, The Club originally had nine members, but over its 30-year existence, membership grew to around 35 and included many of the leading personalities of the period: Goldsmith, David Garrick, Richard Brinsley Sheridan, Adam Smith, the philosopher Edmund Burke (1729–97), and James Boswell (1740–95), author of the *Life of Samuel Johnson* (1791). The Club was 'literary' in the sense of being learned, and members provided each other with support in producing a range of publications in such fields as aesthetics, philosophy, history, musicology, biography, botany and others, as well as works of imaginative literature. Outside The Club, Johnson's circle included many women writers, such as Charlotte Lennox and Frances Burney (1752–1840), to whom he was also generous with support.

3

Critical Approaches

Historical Overview
Current Issues and Debates

HISTORICAL OVERVIEW

In terms of critical reputation, eighteenth-century literature generally fared badly in the century which succeeded it, being widely seen as an arid patch in Britain's literary history between the heights of Shakespeare and Milton and the more recent revivifying achievements of the Romantics. Indeed Romantic poets themselves fuelled a reaction against their immediate forebears. William Wordsworth, for example, objected in his 1800 preface to *Lyrical Ballads* to the 'frantic novels . . . and deluges of idle and extravagant stories in verse' of the last century (Wordsworth 1988, 249), while John Keats (1795–1821) wrote disparagingly in 'Sleep and Poetry' (1817) of the 'foppery and barbarism' of an age in which 'musty laws' dictated literary composition (Keats 2003, 87–8). Later Matthew Arnold complained of the 'provincial and second-rate literature of the eighteenth century' (Arnold 1865, 53), while David Masson (1822–1907), a Scottish critic, summed up a widespread denigration of the period when he asked:

> Is it not one of our commonplaces that 'the Eighteenth Century'
> – and 'the Eighteenth Century' must, in this calculation, be reck-
> oned from about the year 1688, the year of our English

Revolution, to about 1789, the year of the French Revolution –
was, both in Britain, and over the rest of the civilized world, a
century bereft of certain high qualities of heroism, poetry, faith,
or whatever else we may choose to call it, which we do discern in
the mind of previous periods, and distinguished chiefly by a critical and mocking spirit in literature, a superficial and wide-
ranging levity in speculation, and a perseverance reaching to
greatness only in certain tracks of art and of physical science?
(Masson 1859, 82)

Not only the literature but the whole century, then, became
a device within a narrative of progress – a man of straw
against which Victorian commentators could promote an
idea of the higher civilization of their own time.

Reassessment and reclamation of the period arrived in the
early twentieth century, when what had been seen as a lull in
literary achievement became conjoined to a view of the
period's history as a stretch of stability between the Civil War
and the later revolutions, such that a new picture of the literature emerged with emphases upon its responsiveness to and
reflection of a world enjoying a sense of calmness, order and
rationality – a picture encapsulated in the title of George
Saintsbury's *The Peace of the Augustans: A Survey of Eighteenth
Century Literature as a Place of Rest and Refreshment* (1916). The
period's literature appears here as a type of soothing picnic
area in which to recuperate after the rigours of a hectic jolt
through the Renaissance and seventeenth century before
setting off again into the heavy traffic of Romanticism. It
was a comforting grand narrative – one which significantly
emerged around a time of intense European conflict – and it
gained considerable currency, even though when critics such
as Saintsbury addressed specific writers and works there was
actually often little explicit attempt to position them within
that overarching theme.

Critics of the later twentieth century have tended to react
against the generalizations of the peaceful 'Age of Reason'
school and have challenged the exclusivity of the canon of
authors it typically focused upon, so as to produce a 'new eigh-

teenth century' in which plurality and contestation is emphasized over unity and harmony. Where Saintsbury can write of
the century as though it were a single opinionated person ('the
eighteenth century was . . ."bumptious" in its youth . . . it
unluckily did not quite unlearn this bumptiousness in its
middle age' [Saintsbury 1916, 374]), later critics have opened
up a culture of difference and disagreement, bringing in a
wider range of authors and works in the process. In addition
to the broadening of subject matter, movements within literary theory have led to a diversification in terms of approach,
with the burgeoning of so-called 'New Historicist' critical
practices from around 1980 proving to have been particularly
influential. Critics have long examined eighteenth-century literature in relation to contemporary politics, philosophy, religion, aesthetics and so on – there is nothing particularly 'new'
about that – but New Historicist studies have placed greater
emphasis upon the contiguities of imaginative literature and
other discourses and have questioned the boundaries between
them, often suggesting that such boundaries held little sway in
the eighteenth century itself and are the product of later
enterprises through which the idea of 'Literature' as a discrete
category emerged. This has resulted in further shifting of the
canon and of the identity of 'literary studies' as works which
previously might not have been regarded as 'Literature' have
entered literature syllabuses, while works of imaginative literature have been smoothly incorporated into studies of, say,
eighteenth-century medicine or the growth of the British
empire. The field now, therefore, is greatly variegated, and
examined below are just some of the more prominent or
enduring topics and areas of controversy.

CURRENT ISSUES AND DEBATES

The changing canon

Out of the mass of eighteenth-century literary works, which
ones should we read? It is an important question: we are

unable to read everything, so choices have to be made, and sometimes choices regarding appropriate reading will have consequences for large communities of readers – when a literary anthology is being produced, for instance, or when a syllabus for a course of study is being put together. It is also a question which raises further questions concerning the motivation behind the choice: should works be prioritized on the basis of a sense of their literary quality, for example, or because they were popularly read in the eighteenth century itself, or because they uphold a particular political orientation?

Ideas of what constitutes an appropriate canon of eighteenth-century literature have changed radically as different critical approaches and as new political priorities have influenced literary studies. A major revision of the canon began to take place in the 1970s as feminist studies of the period shed new light on numerous neglected women writers, many of whose works have since been republished and become standard reading for anyone interested in the period. Subsequently, powerful cases have been made for the inclusion of other previously marginalized authors and categories of author. Labouring-class writers, for example, now feature more prominently than before on syllabuses and in anthologies. The canon remains a topic of critical discussion and is constantly in a state of revision.

The idea of a canon is also changing in response to new technology and the increasing availability of electronic texts of eighteenth-century works. Before the advent of electronic texts, most readers without access to specialist libraries had their reading matter largely determined by what modern publishers made available. Now, however, an increasing number of readers are able to access a wide range of works electronically, some of which may never have been republished since the eighteenth century. The internet and databases of electronic texts are allowing reading choices to be made with considerably more freedom than before, and are contributing to a greater fluidity in the idea of the canon.

Interest in the canon is also fuelling interrogations of how a canon of eighteenth-century literature originally emerged –

how early anthologies of literature contributed to the prioritization of particular works, and how practices embedded within literary culture began to produce a literary hierarchy. What was the influence upon the canon, for example, of Pope's *Dunciad*, which draws sharp distinctions between gifted and dull writers? Are we still in part the inheritors of Pope's literary judgements? How did early literary reviewing magazines contribute to early canon formation? The canon is not a new issue, but it is still a current one.

The commercialization of literature, new ideas of authorship, and the reading public

Changes in the print market and their impact upon literary production have proven to be of enduring interest to scholars of the period, and a number of interrelated issues relating to authorship, readership, and the mechanisms of the industry continue to attract critical attention. These issues include:

- The expansion of the market for literature and the emergence of the idea of a mass reading public. What was the profile of that reading public? What types of reader – in terms of class, age, sex, location – were reading the various types of literature? How were readers accessing reading material?
- The idea of 'the author'. How did this change as the literary market expanded, and as writers consequently became more distanced from most of their readers? And how did that idea develop in relation to shifts in the economy of the literary world – specifically the growth of a market-based economy alongside an existing system of literary patronage? Throughout the period patrons continued to support some authors, but the influence of patrons lessened as it became possible for 'professional authors' to make livings from the alternative 'patronage' of the paying public.
- How did copyright legislation – introduced in 1710 and later revised and refined – strengthen new conceptions of

authorship? Copyright laws created the notion of literary and intellectual property; the idea of the author as someone with legal rights of ownership over a work was an innovation of the period.

- The emergence of fame within the literary world. The growth of the reading public and the increasing separation of writers from that public fuelled a culture of literary celebrity. Through what types of practice – for example, book reviewing, portraiture, the publication of authors' letters – was celebrity created and sustained? How did celebrity affect literary production and consumption?

Many of these issues, in fact, can be explored with relatively little reference to works of literature. Arguably, though, they are most compelling when seen in relation to actual writing – when they are considered as possible factors which might illuminate why an author wrote in a particular genre, adopted a particular narrative register, chose a particular word, and so on.

Literature, gender and sexuality

The eighteenth century has proven to be a rich field for gender studies, queer theory, and feminist criticism and history, and sex and gender remain a focus of many literary studies. Issues under scrutiny include:

- The representation of different socio-sexual roles within literature.
- The different conditions of authorship for male and female writers.
- The use of literature as a space for promoting models of femininity and masculinity (as, for example, in *Pamela*).
- The representation of non-mainstream sexuality in literature.

Among the most interesting work is that which is examining little-known works concerning sexuality, many of which are gathered in a recent multi-volume anthology of *Eighteenth-Century British Erotica* (2004). Such projects are illuminating an eighteenth-century sexual 'subculture', and with such works to scrutinize as *An Essay upon Improving and Adding to the Strength of Great-Britain and Ireland, by Fornication* (1735) and *Plain Reasons for the Growth of Sodomy in England; to which is added, The Petit Maitre, an odd sort of unpoetic poem, in the trolly-lolly stile* (*c.* 1730), the prospects for the further growth of this field are strong.

The birth/rise/emergence of the novel

This issue has been much debated since the publication in 1957 of Ian Watt's *The Rise of the Novel,* and theories of how the novel came to become such a dominant genre remain very significant within contemporary debates. See 'Prose fiction' in Chapter 2 for further discussion. See also the further reading on prose fiction recommended in Chapter 4 – out of the vast body of novel-focused scholarship, the titles listed have been selected with the principal aim of providing a way into the 'state of play' regarding theories of the novel.

Britishness and regionalism

How did eighteenth-century literary production relate to notions of national identity as they developed after the 1707 union? Following the publication in 1992 of an influential historical study by Linda Colley – *Britons: Forging the Nation, 1707–1837* – there has been a growth in the scholarly interest taken in the processes through which Britishness was 'invented' and transmitted during the eighteenth century. How, critics have asked, did literary works contribute to the shaping of an emergent sense of British national identity? And what role did printed matter have in the dispersal of new ways of thinking about the nation?

   At the same time many scholars are interested in exploring the endurance within Britain of literary regionalism and in examining the separateness of literary traditions and modes of writing within Wales, Scotland and Ireland (and, to some extent, within England). Local nationalism remained alive within the composite nation of Britain, and recent critics have sought to highlight how, for example, the writing of Macpherson and Burns needs to be considered in the context of Scotland and Scottish literary traditions rather than as part of a monolithic British project focused upon the creation of a new nation.

British literature and the wider world

As the globalization phenomenon of our own times attracts more and more attention, critics are increasingly interrogating the prehistory of globalization in the eighteenth century, when empires were growing and when trade and travel were fuelling a new circulation of goods and knowledge around the world. The implications of Britain's internationalism for literature are many and varied, and open up numerous lines of enquiry. For example:

- How were foreign 'others' represented in literature, and what sort of ideologies concerning race informed literary representations?
- What were the mechanisms by which literature came to be circulated internationally?
- How did literary imports from abroad – for example, oriental tales – influence British cultural production? To what extent were imported works transformed, not only linguistically, if they were translated?
- How were British-authored works received when they were read abroad, and what contributions did they make to foreign literary cultures?
- What impact did interests in travel and travel writing have upon the development of literary genres?

Such questions as these are not all new, but they continue to be asked within the ongoing exploration of Britain's complex enmeshment within international culture.

Literature, slavery and the abolition movement

'Britons never will be slaves!' – a line that proud Britons have been able to chorus since 1740 when 'Rule Britannia' by James Thomson and Thomas Arne (1710–78) had its first performance. A great many Britons, though, had no qualms about owning slaves and profiting from them. The Atlantic slave trade played a very significant role in the growth of Britain's economy during the eighteenth century, and the commercial exploitation of vast numbers of West Africans was, for many, justified by the argument that the enslaved peoples were racially inferior to white Europeans – they were seen as somehow less than human – and so were not entitled to be treated in the same way as Europeans. Our period, however, also saw the growth of a powerful abolition movement – a prehistory to the intensified anti-slavery campaign which gathered pace after 1789, the year of an extremely influential abolitionist speech to Parliament by William Wilberforce (1759–1833).

In what ways, recent critics have asked, did literature uphold or justify the slave trade? And in what ways did literature contribute to the campaign to abolish slavery? Or, if abolition seemed too extreme or far-fetched, did literature take part in movements to ameliorate the lot of slaves? A focus upon slavery and abolition has increased the critical attention to the many works by British authors which engage self-consciously with these issues, such as Hannah More's *Slavery, A Poem* (1788) and Anne Yearsley's *A Poem on the Inhumanity of the Slave-Trade* (1788), as well as to the writings of slaves and freed slaves such as Ignatius Sancho (1729–80), whose letters were published in 1782, and Olaudah Equiano (*c.* 1745–97), the author of a best-selling autobiography, *The Interesting Narrative of the Life of Olaudah Equiano, or Gustavus Vassa, the African* (1789). This focus is also producing new enquiries into works which may be silently complicit with or resistant to slavery, or which articulate ambiguous or uncertain positions within the politics of slavery and abolition. What are readers to make of, say, Crusoe's participation in the slave trade and his treatment of his island companion, Friday, in *Robinson Crusoe*? How might these aspects of Defoe's work have been interpreted by early readers? Critics are also exploring the relationship between abolitionism and other discourses – the way in which, for example, the mid-century growth of sentimentalism provided rhetorical strategies for abolitionist argument, as when Sterne introduced an emotive representation of an enchained captive in *A Sentimental Journey* (1768).

4

Resources for Independent Study

Chronology of Key Historical and Cultural Events and Publications
Glossary of Key Terms and Concepts
Further Reading and Resources

CHRONOLOGY OF KEY HISTORICAL AND CULTURAL EVENTS AND PUBLICATIONS

Year	Historical events	Publications and other literary and cultural events
1688	William of Orange lands in England. James II flees to France.	Aphra Behn, *Oroonoko*.
1689	Formal accession of William III and Mary, accompanied by Bill of Rights. Toleration Act grants new rights to Protestant dissenters. Start of Nine Years' War against France.	John Locke, *An Essay Concerning Human Understanding*.
1690	William defeats James's forces in Ireland at Battle of the Boyne.	
1692		William Congreve, *Incognita*.

1693		Congreve, *The Old Batchelor*.
1694	Bank of England founded. Triennial Act establishes elections at least every three years. Death of Queen Mary.	
1695	Bank of Scotland founded.	Lapsing of the press Licensing Act. Congreve, *Love for Love*.
1697	Nine Years' War concluded with the Treaty of Ryswick.	
1698		Jeremy Collier, *A Short View of the Immorality and Profaneness of the English Stage*. George Farquhar, *Love and a Bottle*.
1700		Congreve, *The Way of the World*; Farquhar, *The Constant Couple*; John Dryden, *Fables Ancient and Modern*.
1701	Act of Settlement settles the succession on the house of Hanover.	John Dennis, *The Advancement and Reformation of Modern Poetry*; John Philips, *The Splendid Shilling*;
	War of Spanish Succession begins.	Anne Finch, *The Spleen*; Mary Chudleigh, *The Ladies Defence*.
1702	Death of William III; accession of Queen Anne. England enters War of Spanish Succession.	Nicholas Rowe, *Tamerlane*.
1703		Rowe, *The Fair Penitent*;

		Susannah Centlivre, *Love's Contrivance.*
1704	Duke of Marlborough defeats the French at Battle of Blenheim.	Isaac Newton, *Opticks*; Jonathan Swift, *A Tale of a Tub* and *The Battle of the Books*; first volumes of *The Arabian Nights Entertainment* in English.
1705		Philips, *Blenheim*; Centlivre, *The Gamester.*
1706		Farquhar, *The Recruiting Officer.*
1707	Act of Union joins Scotland with England and Wales.	Farquhar, *The Beaux' Stratagem.*
1708		John Philips, *Cyder.*
1709		Richard Steele and Joseph Addison, *The Tatler* (−1711); Delarivière Manley, *The New Atlantis* and *The Female Tatler*; (−1710) Alexander Pope, *Pastorals*; Matthew Prior, *Poems on Several Occasions*; Centlivre, *The Busie Body.*
1710	Henry Sacheverell impeached. Beginning of Tory ministry under Robert Harley and Henry St John (later Viscount Bolingbroke).	Copyright Act grants authors legal ownership of their works for 14 years following publication. Swift, 'A Description of a City Shower'.
1711	Completion of St Paul's Cathedral. Founding of the South Sea Company.	Steele and Addison, *The Spectator* (−1712; revived in 1714); Pope, *An Essay on Criticism*;

		Anthony Ashley Cooper, Third Earl of Shaftesbury, *Characteristicks of Men, Manners, Opinions, Times*; George Frederick Handel, *Rinaldo*.
1712		Pope, *The Rape of the Lock* (2 canto version).
1713	War of Spanish Succession ends with Treaty of Utrecht.	Addison, *Cato*; Pope, *Windsor Forest*; John Gay, *Rural Sports*; Finch, *Miscellany Poems on Several Occasions*; Thomas Parnell, *An Essay on the Different Styles of Poetry*.
1714	Death of Queen Anne; accession of George I. End of Tory ministry; beginning of long Whig domination.	Bernard de Mandeville, *The Fable of the Bees* (–1729); Rowe, *The Tragedy of Jane Shore*; Centlivre, *The Wonder: A Woman Keeps a Secret*; Pope, *The Rape of the Lock* (expanded version).
1715	Failed Jacobite uprising in support of the 'Old Pretender', 'James III'.	*The Iliad of Homer* translated by Pope (–1720).
1716	Septennial Act extends period between elections to maximum of seven years.	Gay, *Trivia; or, the Art of Walking the Streets of London*; Lady Mary Wortley Montagu, 'Town Eclogues'.
1717	Bishop Benjamin Hoadly brings about the 'Bangorian Controversy'.	*The Works of Mr. Alexander Pope*.
1718		Centlivre, *A Bold Stroke*

		for a Wife; Matthew Prior, *Poems on Several Occasions.*
1719		Daniel Defoe, *Robinson Crusoe*; Eliza Haywood, *Love in Excess.*
1720	The 'South Sea Bubble' stock market crash.	Gay, *Poems on Several Occasions.*
1721	Robert Walpole becomes First Lord of the Treasury.	
1722	The 'Atterbury Plot': an attempted Jacobite uprising.	Defoe, *Moll Flanders*; Parnell, *Poems on Several Occasions*; Steele, *The Conscious Lovers.*
1723		*A Collection of Old Ballads.*
1724		Swift, *The Drapier's Letters*; Defoe, *A Tour Thro. the Whole Island of Great Britain.*
1725		Francis Hutcheson, *An Inquiry into the Original of our Ideas of Beauty and Virtue*; *The Odyssey of Homer* translated by Pope (–1726).
1726		Swift, *Gulliver's Travels*; John Dyer, *Grongar Hill.*
1727	Death of George I; accession of George II.	Gay, *Fables* (first series); Thomson, *To the Memory of Newton*; Pope, *Peri Bathous, or Of the Art of Sinking in Poetry.*
1728		Gay, *The Beggar's Opera*; Pope, *The Dunciad.*
1729		Swift, *A Modest Proposal*; Pope, *The Dunciad Variorum*; Richard Savage, *The Wanderer.*

1730		James Thomson, *The Seasons*; Stephen Duck, *Poems on Several Subjects*.
1731		Foundation of the *Gentleman's Magazine* (–1907); George Lillo, *The London Merchant*; Pope, *An Epistle to Burlington* (–1744).
1732	Opening of revamped Vauxhall Gardens.	William Hogarth, 'A Harlot's Progress'; Swift, 'The Lady's Dressing Room'; Pope, *Epistle to Bathurst*.
1733	Walpole's unpopular customs and excise reorganization causes 'The Excise Crisis'.	Pope, *An Essay on Man* (–1734); Hogarth, 'The Rake's Progress'.
1735		Pope, *An Epistle to Dr Arbuthnot* and *An Epistle to a Lady*; Thomson, *Liberty*.
1736	Witchcraft Act forbids accusations of sorcery. The Gin Act raises the price of gin and causes rioting.	Henry Fielding, *Pasquin, A Dramatic Satire on the Times*.
1737	Death of Queen Caroline.	Theatrical Licensing Act. *The Historical Register for the Year 1736*; John and Charles Wesley, *A Collection of Psalms and Hymns*.
1738	Beginning of Methodism as John Wesley's experiences a spiritual conversion.	Samuel Johnson, *London*.
1739	'War of Jenkins' Ear'	Swift, *Verses on the Death*

	against Spain.	*of Dr. Swift*; David Hume, *A Treatise of Human Nature*; Mary Collier, 'The Woman's Labour'.
1740	War of the Austrian Succession begins.	Samuel Richardson, *Pamela* (–1742); Thomson and Thomas Arne, *Alfred: A Masque* (featuring 'Rule Britannia').
1741	Britain drawn into War of the Austrian Succession.	David Garrick's London stage debut. Fielding, *Shamela*; Handel, *The Messiah*; Hume, *Essays, Moral and Political*.
1742	End of Walpole's primacy.	Fielding, *Joseph Andrews*; Pope, *New Dunciad*; Edward Young, *Night Thoughts* (–1745).
1743		Robert Blair, *The Grave*; Pope, *The Dunciad in Four Books*; Fielding, *Jonathan Wild*; Hogarth, *Marriage à-la-Mode*.
1744		Mark Akenside, *The Pleasures of Imagination*; Sarah Fielding, *David Simple* (–1753); Haywood, *The Female Spectator* (–1746); Johnson, *Life of Savage*.
1745	Jacobite uprising led by Charles Edward Stuart, the 'Young Pretender'.	Akenside, *Odes on Several Subjects*.
1746	Defeat of Jacobites at the Battle of Culloden.	Joseph Warton, *Odes on Various Subjects*.

1747		Richardson, *Clarissa* (–1748); Thomas Gray, *Ode on a Distant Prospect of Eton College*; Johnson, *Plan of a Dictionary of the English Language*.
1748	War of the Austrian Succession concludes with Treaty of Aix-la-Chapelle.	John Cleland, *Memoirs of a Woman of Pleasure* (–1749); Tobias Smollett, *Roderick Random*; Mary Leapor, *Poems upon Several Occasions*; Thomson, *The Castle of Indolence*; Hume, *An Enquiry concerning Human Understanding*.
1749		Fielding, *Tom Jones*; Johnson, *The Vanity of Human Wishes*. Launch of the *Monthly Review*.
1750	Earthquake in London.	Johnson, *Rambler* (–1752).
1751	Death of Frederick, Prince of Wales.	Gray, *Elegy Written in a Country Churchyard*; Fielding, *Amelia*; Haywood, *Betsy Thoughtless*; Smollett, *Peregrine Pickle*.
1752	Britain adopts the Gregorian calendar.	Charlotte Lennox, *The Female Quixote*; Christopher Smart, *Poems on Several Occasions*.
1753	Jewish Naturalization Act. Founding of the British Museum.	Richardson, *Sir Charles Grandison* (–1754); Hogarth, *The Analysis of Beauty*.
1755	Huge earthquake destroys much of Lisbon.	Johnson, *A Dictionary of the English Language*.

1756 Start of the Seven Years' War with France.

Launch of the *Critical Review*.

1757

Edmund Burke, *A Philosophical Enquiry into the Origin of Our Ideas of the Sublime and Beautiful*; John Dyer, *The Fleece*; Gray, *Odes*.

1758

Johnson, *The Idler* (–1760).

1759 Britain wins military victories in Canada, India, Germany and the West Indies, and gains naval supremacy through-out much of the world. British Museum opens to the public. Foundation of Josiah Wedgwood's pottery works.

Johnson, *Rasselas*; Laurence Sterne, *Tristram Shandy* (–1767); Charles Macklin, *Love à la Mode*; Adam Smith, *The Theory of Moral Sentiments*.

1760 Death of George II; accession of George III.

James Macpherson, *Fragments of Ancient Poetry*; Charles Johnstone, *Chrysal; or, The Adventures of a Guinea* (–1765); Smollett, *Sir Launcelot Greaves* (–1761).

1761

Frances Sheridan, *Sidney Bidulph*; Charles Churchill, *The Rosciad*.

1762

Mary Collier, *Poems on Several Occasions*; Macpherson, *Fingal, an Ancient Epic Poem*; Oliver Goldsmith, *The Citizen of the World*.

1763 Seven Years' War concluded with Treaty

Hugh Blair, *A Critical Dissertation on the Poems*

of Paris. John Wilkes's *North Briton* No. 45 rouses popular protest.

1764 Invention of the 'spinning jenny' by James Hargreaves.

1765 The Stamp Act imposes taxes on American documents, increasing opposition to the government in the colonies.

1766

1768 James Cook's first voyage to Australia and New Zealand (–1771). Supporters of Wilkes killed at St George's Fields Massacre. Founding of the Royal Academy of Arts.

1769 Patenting of James Watt's steam engine.

1770

1771 Richard Arkwright's

of Ossian; Frances Brooke, *Julia Mandeville*.

Horace Walpole, *The Castle of Otranto*; James Grainger, *The Sugar-Cane*. Wolfgang Amadeus Mozart presented as a musical prodigy in England. Thomas Percy, *Reliques of Ancient English Poetry*.

Goldsmith, *The Vicar of Wakefield*; Smollett, *Travels through France and Italy*.

Sterne, *A Sentimental Journey through France and Italy*; Hugh Kelly, *The False Delicacy*. Launch of the *Encyclopaedia Britannica*.

Shakespeare Jubilee arranged by Garrick. Joshua Reynolds begins presenting annual *Discourses on Art* (–1790). Richard Cumberland, *The Brothers*.

Goldsmith, *The Deserted Village*.

Smollett, *Humphry*

first water-powered spinning mill opens.

Clinker; Henry Mackenzie, *The Man of Feeling*; Cumberland, *The West Indian*.

1772 Cook's second voyage (–1775).

Samuel Foote, *The Nabob*.

1773 The 'Boston Tea Party'.

Oliver Goldsmith, *She Stoops to Conquer*; Anna Laetitia Barbauld, *Poems*.

1774 Joseph Priestley discovers oxygen.

Thomas Warton, *History of English Poetry* (–1781).

1775 Start of American War of Independence.

Richard Brinsley Sheridan, *The Rivals*; Johnson, *Journey to the Western Islands of Scotland*.

1776 American Declaration of Independence. Cook's third voyage (–1779).

Smith, *The Wealth of Nations*; Edward Gibbon, *The Decline and Fall of the Roman Empire* (–1788).

1777

Sheridan, *The School for Scandal*; Thomas Chatterton, *Poems*; Thomas Warton, *Poems*.

1778 Catholic Relief Act.

Frances Burney, *Evelina*.

1779 Construction of the first iron bridge.

Johnson, *Lives of the English Poets* (–1781); Sheridan, *The Critic*; Hume, *Dialogues concerning Natural Religion*.

1780 Protestant opposition to Catholic Relief Act leads to the 'Gordon Riots'.

1782

William Cowper, *Poems*; Burney, *Cecilia*; Ignatius Sancho, *Letters*.

1783 War of American

George Crabbe, *The*

	Independence ended with Treaties of Paris and Versailles.	*Village.*
1784	East India Act reduces the East India Company's autonomy in India and gives the government greater control.	Charlotte Smith, *Elegiac Sonnets*.
1785	Edmund Cartwright's steam-powered loom patented. First balloon flight across English Channel.	Cowper, *The Task*; Anne Yearsley, *Poems on Several Occasions*; James Boswell, *Journal of a Tour to the Hebrides*.
1786		Robert Burns, *Poems, Chiefly in the Scottish Dialect*; Helen Maria Williams, *Poems*; William Beckford, *Vathek*.
1787	Signing of the US Constitution. Society for Effecting the Abolition of the Slave Trade founded.	Mary Wollstonecraft, *Thoughts on the Education of Daughters*.
1788	George III's illness causes the 'Regency Crisis' within government.	Hannah More, *Slavery, A Poem*; Yearsley, *A Poem on the Inhumanity of the Slave-Trade*; Wollstonecraft, *Mary*.
1789	Start of the French Revolution; fall of the Bastille.	Olaudah Equiano, *The Interesting Narrative of the Life of Olaudah Equiano*; William Blake, *Songs of Innocence*.

GLOSSARY OF KEY TERMS AND CONCEPTS

Augustan

A term sometimes applied to literature from the late seventeenth to the mid-eighteenth century – particularly the works of Dryden, Pope, Swift and Johnson. It invokes such writers' admiration and imitation of the ancient Latin authors – particularly Virgil, Horace and Ovid – who flourished during the reign of the emperor Augustus (27BC–14AD). Suggesting that the writing of Pope *et al.* can be characterized by a neoclassical urbanity, use of the term in phrases such as 'the Augustan Age' has become less common in recent eighteenth-century studies as scholars have tended to become wary of totalizing visions of the era.

Ballad opera

A musical dramatic genre developed and popularized primarily by John Gay with *The Beggar's Opera*, which interweaves dialogue with songs set to popular tunes. In Gay's hands, the form became associated with championing the common people, and his sequel *Polly* (1729) was initially banned from the stage for its provocative political content. A forerunner of the modern stage musical, later eighteenth-century examples include Richard Brinsley Sheridan's *The Duenna* (1775).

Broadside

A single-sheet publication, usually printed on just one side of the paper, and often sold cheaply by hawkers. Popular ballads and songs were commonly published in this form – hence the term 'broadside ballad' – but broadsides were also used for the dissemination of a wide range of short texts including news reports, announcements and speeches.

Coffeehouse

From the mid-seventeenth century there was a proliferation of coffeehouses in London (estimates suggest that by 1740 there were well over 500 in the capital). Typically they were informal meeting places where a predominantly male clientele would drink coffee (or chocolate), smoke, converse and read. They were important to literary culture as venues where literary works could be distributed, exchanged and discussed, but they also came to shape certain literary forms, particularly the periodical essay (see 'Periodicals and periodical essays' in Chapter 2). As sites where public discourse was generated and transmitted, coffeehouses have been seen as essential components within the 'public sphere'.

Enlightenment

This term is sometimes used to designate the eighteenth century as a whole, but it is more specifically associated with intellectual movements of the period (particularly those taking place in France) which promoted the systematic application of reason in order to discover knowledge of human life and to improve human existence through the development of new social and political systems. The term was not widely used at the time, but gained in currency from the late nineteenth century. It is typically used to embrace the projects of a wide range of intellectuals – in science, philosophy and political thought – with shared beliefs in the idea of the universe as a system controlled by discernible laws and in the idea of human progress. Promoting non-authoritarian systems of social organization, Enlightenment thought is seen to have fuelled the French and American revolutions.

Epistolary novel

A type of fiction in which the story is conveyed through letters supposedly written by the characters. The form is not unique to the eighteenth century, but it was much used by eighteenth-century writers, including Aphra Behn, Samuel Richardson, Tobias Smollett and Frances Burney, all of whom exploited the capacity of the form to present readers with multiple narrative viewpoints. In some epistolary novels, the letters are not only the vehicle of the story, but are important elements *within* the story, as in Richardson's *Clarissa* in which the epistolary communication between characters –

involving covert letters, hidden letters and so on – contributes to the development of the plot.

Gothic

Within the field of architecture, 'gothic' refers to the medieval style of building (particularly of churches and castles), of which there was a significant revival in the eighteenth century. Among the best-known 'gothic revival' buildings of the period is 'Strawberry Hill' at Twickenham – the architectural plaything of Horace Walpole, who had his house adapted and extended in the style of a gothic castle in several phases from 1747. Walpole was also a pioneer of literary gothicism, a type of writing which aims to provide readers with 'pleasing terror' by means of suspenseful tales filled with mysteries, threatening settings, and very often supernatural events and creatures. As in architecture, literary gothicism made extensive reference to medieval matters: Walpole's *The Castle of Otranto* purports to be a medieval tale, and many subsequent gothic works invoked this past – for example, by employing medieval castles and monasteries as settings – even when their stories take place in contemporary times. Another gothic fiction falling within our period was *Vathek* (1786) by William Beckford (1759–1844), which contributed to a significant growth in the popularity of the genre in the 1790s.

Graveyard poetry

A type of poetry presenting melancholic reflections on mortality, framed in narratives involving visits to graveyards and other reminders of death. The most celebrated examples of this type of verse were published in the mid-century and include Edward Young's *The Complaint; or, Night Thoughts on Life, Death, and Immortality* (1742–45), Robert Blair's *The Grave* (1743) and Thomas Gray's *Elegy Written in a Country Churchyard* (1751). With its personal and introspective concerns, such verse has been seen as significant as part of a transitional phase between publicly focused neoclassical verse and Romantic lyricism, but it is of interest not only as a stepping-stone in literary history. Involving a focus upon loss, and with extensive analyses of feeling, such verse played a part in the wider culture of sensibility.

Grub Street

This was the name of an actual street in the city of London, as well as a symbolic location for the culture of low-level, market-driven 'hack' authorship created by the commercialization of the publishing industry. Johnson's *Dictionary* describes it as a street 'much inhabited by writers of small histories, dictionaries, and temporary poems; whence any mean production is called *grubstreet*'. Grub Street writers and their works are derided in Pope's *The Dunciad* and Swift's *A Tale of a Tub*, but many writers who claimed to occupy more elevated literary ground – including Pope and Swift – were themselves no strangers to the commercial pressures represented by Grub Street. The idea of Grub Street served as a reference point for asserting distinctions between 'high' and 'low' literature, but actual divisions were very blurred.

Heroic couplet

A poetic unit comprised of a rhyming pair of pentameter lines, almost always with an underlying iambic rhythm and usually with ten syllables in each line. Never more popular than in the late seventeenth and eighteenth centuries, such couplets were employed by numerous writers including John Dryden, Alexander Pope, Lady Mary Wortley Montagu, Stephen Duck, Mary Collier, Samuel Johnson, Oliver Goldsmith, and George Crabbe (1754–1832). (See 'Poetry – Poetic forms: traditions and innovations' in Chapter 2.)

Man of feeling

A male character type associated with sentimental fiction. Men of feeling are sensitive beings with an attraction to scenes of distress which often move them to tears and provoke them to perform benevolent actions to relieve the distress. Typically unworldly, they are regularly preyed upon in fiction by characters seeking to exploit their ready benevolence: they demonstrate the 'moral sense' described by Shaftesbury, but are often surrounded by characters with Hobbesian self-interest (see 'Religion, Science and Philosophy – Explorations in thought' in Chapter 1). Well-known examples include the eponymous hero of Sarah Fielding's *David Simple* and Harley in Henry Mackenzie's *The Man of Feeling*. Yorick in Sterne's *A Sentimental Journey* is a more complex man of feeling, with an erotic drive often absent from the type.

Mock-epic and mock-heroic

The mock-epic is a literary form in which conventions of classical epic writing, such as grandiose language, heroic conflicts, invocations to the gods and supernatural machinery, are employed in the description of commonplace characters and events. It plays upon a deliberate mismatch between style and content and is almost always employed for satirical purposes. One of the most admired examples of mock-epic is Pope's *The Rape of the Lock*, written in response to an argument between two families which arose when a young male aristocrat cut a lock of hair from a society beauty. The poem wryly represents the squabble as though it were a major historical event; it employs grand invocations, for instance, and presents a game of cards with language and imagery appropriate to the narration of heroic battles. In this poem, as in other mock-epics, there is a comic trivialization of the subject matter, but mock-epic does not only trivialize. In fact, the serious mode of representation can have the effect of making trivial matters seem important; there is, for example, some sense of serious tragedy in *The Rape of the Lock* amidst the satire.

Mock-heroic is closely related to mock-epic, but is generally used in a wider sense to refer to any literature that ridicules its subject by means of an inappropriately exaggerated treatment, which often produces a sense of bathos. More than mock-epic, mock-heroic is also associated with burlesque and parodic writing – comic forms where a literary style rather than an element of content is the main object of satire.

Periodical

A regularly published journal or magazine – a form of publication which burgeoned from the late seventeenth century (see 'Periodicals and periodical essays' in Chapter 2).

Public sphere

The idea of the 'public sphere', or the 'bourgeois public sphere', has been influential within English-language eighteenth-century studies since the 1990s. It derives from a work by the philosopher Jürgen Habermas (b. 1929), published in German in 1962 and later translated into English (Habermas, 1989). The term refers to the network of channels and sites of communication which allows for the creation of public opinion and allows for public opinion to gain a degree of influence, despite it having no official status within political discourse. Habermas locates the origins of the 'public sphere' in the expanding communication network of early eighteenth-century Britain – in the coffeehouses and other meeting places and in the channels of print that emerged from and were consumed in these public locations. How well the model matches the reality, and the extent to which public opinion did translate into political influence, are matters of debate.

Realism

This is an extremely flexible term which is used in many different, sometimes contradictory ways within philosophy and criticism of literature and other art forms. The concept of realism – and use of the term – is complicated in part because different matters are often enmeshed within it: the *mode* of representation, the *matter* being represented (which can be fictional, or can actually exist in the non-literary world), and the effect upon readers (some critics have dubbed works 'realist' if they cause readers/audiences/viewers to reflect upon reality, even if the work does not directly mediate a knowable reality). In relation to the eighteenth century, 'realism' is mostly used in discussions of prose fiction to refer to a type of writing in which nature or contemporary life is depicted in recognizable detail and with fidelity. The realist mode, then, stands in contrast to idealized depictions of the world, and other modes of representation in which the nature of things is exaggerated or presented in some form of guise. 'Realism' has commonly been seen as a defining feature of the innovative works of fiction produced by Daniel Defoe, Henry Fielding and Samuel Richardson – as a feature which marks these works out as 'novels' and sets them apart from 'romances' (see 'Prose fiction – The rise of the "familiar" and the plausible' in Chapter 2). Due to the problematic nature of the term, some critics have questioned its usefulness and prefer to steer clear of it.

Sentiment, sentimental and sensibility

See 'Religion, Science and Philosophy – Explorations in thought' in Chapter 1, and the ongoing discussion of sentimentalism's manifestation in the different genres of literature in Chapter 2.

FURTHER READING AND RESOURCES

Cultural and historical context

Barker-Benfield, G. J. (1992), *The Culture of Sensibility: Sex and Society in Eighteenth-Century Britain*. Chicago: University of Chicago Press. A significant gender-focused study of the rise of sensibility and the sentimental.

Brewer, John (1989), *The Sinews of Power: War, Money and the English State, 1688–1783*. Cambridge, MA: Harvard University Press. Presents a forceful argument for the 'military-fiscal' basis of the nation's growth as an international power.

Clark, J. C. D. (1985), *English Society, 1688–1832: Ideology, Social Structure and Political Practice During the Ancien Regime*. Cambridge: Cambridge University Press. An argument for the ongoing conservatism of a society structured by the monarchy, aristocracy and the Church – a check against over-zealous accounts of the period's modernity and emerging liberalism.

Colley, Linda (1992), *Britons: Forging the Nation, 1707–1837*. New Haven, CT: Yale University Press. An extremely influential study of the making of the nation and of the idea of Britain following the Act of Union.

Langford, Paul (1989), *A Polite and Commercial People: England, 1727–1783*. Oxford: Oxford University Press. An account of the century's middle years, which emphasizes growing middle-class prosperity and self-confidence as fundamental to national developments.

O'Gorman, Frank (1987), *The Long Eighteenth Century: British Political and Social History, 1688–1832*. London: Arnold. A balanced and detailed account of politics and society up to the Reform Acts – readable and reliable. An excellent starting-point.

Porter, Roy (1982), *English Society in the Eighteenth Century*. London: Allen Lane. A fast-paced, wide-ranging survey of English society, both 'high' and 'low'.

Thompson, E. P. (1991), *Customs in Common: Studies in Traditional Popular Culture*. London: Merlin Press. An analysis of cultural practices and rituals among the lower orders and of the causes and meanings they embodied.

Wilson, Kathleen (1995), *The Sense of the People: Politics, Culture and Imperialism in England, 1715–1785*. Cambridge: Cambridge University Press. Examines extra-parliamentary politics and the role of imperialism within the emergence of a national consciousness.

General literature and authorship

Donoghue, Frank (1996), *The Fame Machine: Book Reviewing and Eighteenth-Century Literary Careers*. Stanford, CA: Stanford University Press. Plots the emergence of literary celebrity within the culture of reading and reviewing, with case studies of individual authors.

Feather, John (1985), *The Provincial Book Trade in Eighteenth-Century England*. Cambridge: Cambridge University Press. A pioneering study of the growth of literary culture outside the capital.

—— (1988), *A History of British Publishing*. London: Routledge. An excellent account of printing and publishing from Caxton to the twentieth century; Part Two addresses the industry from 1695 to 1800.

Griffin, Dustin (1996), *Literary Patronage in England, 1650–1800*. Cambridge: Cambridge University Press. Examines the ongoing system of patronage within the developing market economy of print.

Hammond, Brean (1997), *Professional Imaginative Writing in England, 1670–1740: 'Hackney for Bread'*. Oxford: Clarendon Press. A sharp study of how the idea of the professional author emerged.

Rivers, Isabel (ed.) (1982), *Books and their Readers in Eighteenth-Century England*. Leicester: Leicester University Press. An influential collection of essays on book history and literary consumption.

Rogers, Pat (1972), *Grub Street: Studies in a Subculture*. London: Methuen. A classic study of the hack side of the eighteenth-century print trade, which provides numerous insights into London life along the way.

Speck, W. A. (1998), *Literature and Society in Eighteenth-Century England: Ideology, Politics and Culture, 1680–1820*. London and New York: Longman. An informative account of the relations between literature and ideology in the period.

Todd, Janet (1989), *The Sign of Angellica: Women, Writing and Fiction, 1660–1800*. London: Virago. A classic feminist study of female authorship and images of women authors.

Turner, Cheryl (1992), *Living by the Pen: Women Writers in the Eighteenth Century*. London and New York: Routledge. A study of the conditions of authorship for female writers.

Womersley, David (ed.) (2001), *A Companion to Literature from Milton to Blake*. Oxford: Blackwell. A large multi-disciplinary collection of essays – good for dipping into when the need arises rather than for reading straight through.

Poetry

Christmas, William J. (2001), *The Lab'ring Muses: Work, Writing and the Social Order in English Plebeian Poetry, 1730–1830*. Newark, DE: University of Delaware Press; London: Associated University Presses. Studies poetic production from the lower orders.

Fairer, David (2003), *English Poetry of the Eighteenth Century 1700–1789*. London: Longman. An outstanding overview and an admirable demonstration of what informed reading can elicit from eighteenth-century verse – highly recommended.

Fairer, David, and Christine Gerrard (eds) (1999), *Eighteenth-Century Poetry: An Annotated Anthology*. Oxford: Blackwell. An excellent collection with enlightening editorial material – a very good gateway to the period's verse.

Ferguson, Moira (1995), *Eighteenth-Century Women Poets: Nation, Class, and Gender*. Albany NY: SUNY Press. A feminist study of female-authored verse.

Sitter, John (ed.) (2001), *The Cambridge Companion to Eighteenth-Century Poetry*. Cambridge: Cambridge University Press. A wide-ranging collection of essays addressing the forms, cultural position, politics and authorship of poetry by leading scholars in the field.

Weinbrot, Howard D. (1993), *Britannia's Issue: The Rise of British Literature from Dryden to Ossian*. Cambridge: Cambridge University Press. Examines ways in which British writers rejected classical models and developed a native literature.

Drama

Bevis, Richard W. (1988), *English Drama: Restoration and Eighteenth Century, 1660–1789*. London: Longman. A useful introductory survey.

Brown, Laura (1981), *English Dramatic Form, 1660–1760: An Essay in Generic History*. New Haven and London: Yale University Press. A sophisticated study of the evolution of drama as it developed from a predominantly aristocratic form into a vehicle of bourgeois ideology.

Hughes, Derek (1996), *English Drama, 1660–1700*. Oxford: Oxford University Press. Provides critical readings of a huge number of plays within a clear, well-organized argument; a valuable work on the early drama of the period.

Hume, Robert D. (ed.) (1980), *The London Theatre World, 1660–1800*. Carbondale and Edwardsville: Southern Illinois Press. A collection of essays mapping the theatre world's various provinces.

Thomas, David (ed.) (1989), *Restoration and Georgian England,*

1660–1788 (Theatre in Europe: A Documentary History). Cambridge: Cambridge University Press. A well-chosen collection of eighteenth-century texts with useful introductory and editorial material which illuminates many facets of the theatre world.

Prose fiction

Hammond, Brean, and Shaun Regan, (2006), *Making the Novel: Fiction and Society in Britain, 1660–1789*. Basingstoke: Palgrave Macmillan. A valuable introduction to the fiction of the period and to debates concerning the novel's emergence; the opening sections provide particularly useful orientation.

Hunter, J. Paul (1990), *Before Novels: The Cultural Contexts of Eighteenth-Century Fiction*. New York: W. W. Norton. An extremely readable and erudite account of early prose fiction, emphasizing its relations to 'subliterary' genres, such as newspaper journalism and biography.

Richetti, John (ed.) (1996), *The Cambridge Companion to the Eigheenth-Century Novel*. Cambridge: Cambridge University Press. A useful collection of essays addressing the major subgenres and authors.

Spencer, Jane (1986), *The Rise of the Woman Novelist: from Aphra Behn to Jane Austen*. Oxford: Blackwell. An influential study which has done much to increase the critical attention given to female novelists.

—— (2000), *Reconsidering the Rise of the Novel*, special issue of *Eighteenth-Century Fiction*, 12 (2–3). An important collection of essays by leading writers on the novel's emergence, reflecting upon the impact of Watt's *Rise of the Novel* and upon the future of novel studies.

Warner, William B. (1998), *Licensing Entertainment: The Elevation of Novel Reading in Britain, 1684–1750*. Berkeley: University of California Press. Examines the increasing legitimacy of the novel in relation to developing ideas of reading, and includes an informative discussion of the evolution of the whole 'rise of the novel' debate.

Watt, Ian (1957), *The Rise of the Novel: Studies in Defoe, Richardson and*

Fielding. London: Chatto & Windus. A seminal work for modern debates concerning the novel genre and its emergence.

Other resources

There are numerous websites devoted to different aspects of eighteenth-century literature and culture. Links to many of the best are found at the following page:

http://andromeda.rutgers.edu/~jlynch/18th/

Two subscription-based online databases, both fully searchable, provide access to a wealth of eighteenth-century texts:

Chadwyck-Healey's *Literature Online*. This also provides introductions to many of the major eighteenth-century authors, as well as access to critical material.

Thomson Gale's *Eighteenth Century Collections Online* (ECCO). This is an enormous database (around 26 million pages of material apparently), and is particularly useful for it presents digitized images of the original texts.

Works Cited

The following list presents editions of works actually quoted or drawn upon directly in the main text; it does not include works which are only mentioned. Dates given here are for the editions used; first edition dates are given in the main text.

Addison, Joseph (1713), *Cato. A Tragedy*. London: J. Tonson.

Anon. (1733), *The Congress of Excise-Asses, Or, Sir B--ue S--ng's Overthrow: A New Ballad*. London.

Anon. (1796), *The Monthly Magazine* (October).

Arnold, Matthew (1865), *Essays in Criticism*. London and Cambridge: Macmillan.

Arnold, Matthew (1970), *Selected Prose*. P. J. Keating (ed.). Harmondsworth: Penguin Books.

Behn, Aphra (1992), *Oroonoko, The Rover and Other Works*. J. Todd (ed.). London: Penguin Books.

Bond, Donald F. (ed.) (1965), *The Spectator*. 5 vols. Oxford: Clarendon Press.

Boswell, James (1980), *Life of Johnson*. Ed. R. W. Chapman. Rev. J. D. Fleeman. Oxford: Oxford University Press.

Brissenden, R. F. (1974), *Virtue in Distress: Studies in the Novel of Sentiment from Richardson to Sade*. London: Macmillan.

Centlivre, Susannah (1703), *Love's Contrivance*. London: Bernard Lintott.

Chippendale, Thomas (1754), *The Gentleman and Cabinet-Maker's Director*. London: printed for the author.

Collier, Jeremy (1974), *A Short View of the Immorality and Profaneness of the English Stage*. New York: AMS Press.

Colvill, Robert (1747), *Britain, A Poem*. Edinburgh: Ruddiman.

Congreve, William (1692), *Incognita; or, Love and Duty Reconcil'd.* London.

Davies, Thomas (1780), *Memoirs of the Life of David Garrick.* 2 vols. London.

Defoe, Daniel (1994), *Robinson Crusoe.* M. Shinagel (ed.). 2nd edn. New York and London: W. W. Norton.

Fairer, David, and Christine Gerrard, (eds) (1999), *Eighteenth-Century Poetry: An Annotated Anthology.* Oxford: Blackwell.

Farquhar, George (1988), *The Works of George Farquhar.* 2 vols. S. S. Kenny (ed.). Oxford: Clarendon Press.

Gay, John (1728), *The Beggar's Opera.* London: John Watts.

Goldsmith, Oliver (1966), *Collected Works of Oliver Goldsmith.* 5 vols. Arthur Friedman (ed.). Oxford: Clarendon Press.

Habermas, Jürgen (1989), *The Structural Transformation of the Public Sphere: An Inquiry into a Category of Bourgeois Society.* Thomas Burger (trans.). Cambridge: Polity Press.

Haywood, Eliza (1745), *The Female Spectator.* 4 vols. London: T. Gardner.

Hume, David (1742), *Essays, Moral and Political.* 2 vols. Edinburgh: A. Kincaid.

Johnson, Samuel (1755), *A Dictionary of the English Language.* 2 vols. London: Strahan *et al.*

—— (1905), *Lives of the English Poets.* 3 vols. George Birkbeck Hill (ed.). Oxford: Clarendon Press.

—— (1963), *The Idler and The Adventurer.* Vol. II of *The Yale Edition of the Works of Samuel Johnson.* W. J. Bate, J. M. Bullitt and L. F. Powell (eds). New Haven and London: Yale University Press.

—— (1969), *The Rambler.* Vols III–V of *The Yale Edition of the Works of Samuel Johnson.* W. J. Bate and Albrecht B. Strauss (eds). New Haven and London: Yale University Press.

Keats, John (2003), *The Complete Poems.* John Barnard (ed.). Updated 3rd edn. London: Penguin Books.

Lennox, Charlotte (1989), *The Female Quixote; or, The Adventures of Arabella.* Margaret Dalziel (ed.). Oxford: Oxford University Press.

Locke, John (1721), *An Essay Concerning Human Understanding . . . Eighth Edition, with large Additions.* 2 vols. London: A. Churchill and A. Manship.

Mandeville, Bernard de (1714), *The Fable of the Bees; or, Private Vices Publick Benefits*. London: J. Roberts.

Martyn, Thomas (1766), *The English Connoisseur: Containing An Account of Whatever is Curious in Painting, Sculpture, &c. In the Palaces and Seats of the Nobility and Principal Gentry of England, Both in Town and Country*. 2 vols. London: L. Davis and C. Reymers.

Masson, David (1859), *British Novelists and their Styles*. Cambridge: Macmillan.

Milton, John (1997), *Paradise Lost*. A. Fowler (ed.). London and New York: Longman.

Moritz, Karl Phillip (1795), *Travels, Chiefly on Foot, Through Several Parts of England, in 1782*. London: G. G. and J. Robinson.

Nugent, Thomas (1756), *The Grand Tour; or, A Journey through the Netherlands, Germany, Italy and France*. 2nd edn. 4 vols. London: D. Browne *et al.*

O'Gorman, F. (1997), *The Long Eighteenth Century: British Political and Social History, 1688–1832*. London: Arnold.

Pope, Alexander (1735), *The Works of Alexander Pope*. 2 vols. London: Gilliver.

—— (2006), *The Major Works*. Pat Rogers (ed.). Oxford: Oxford University Press.

Richardson, Samuel (1965), *Pamela; or, Virtue Rewarded*. 2 vols. Mark Kinkead-Weekes (ed.). London: Dent.

—— (2001), *Pamela; or, Virtue Rewarded*. Thomas Keymer and Alice Wakely (eds). Oxford: Oxford University Press.

Rochester, John Wilmot (1984), *The Poems of John Wilmot, Earl of Rochester*. K. Walker (ed.). Oxford: Blackwell.

Rowe, Nicholas (1756), *The Works of Nicholas Rowe*. 2 vols. London: J. and R. Tonson *et al.*

Saintsbury, George (1916), *The Peace of the Augustans: A Survey of Eighteenth Century Literature as a Place of Rest and Refreshment*. London: G. Bell.

Sheridan, Frances (1761), *Memoirs of Miss Sidney Bidulph*. 3 vols. London: R. and J. Dodsley.

Smith, Adam (1776), *An Inquiry into the Nature and Causes of the Wealth of Nations*. 2 vols. London: W. Strahan and T. Cadell.

Steele, Richard (1723), *The Conscious Lovers. A Comedy*. London: J. Tonson.

Swift, Jonathan (2001), *Gulliver's Travels*. R. DeMaria Jr (ed.). London: Penguin Books.

Thomas, Peter D. G. (2002), *George III: King and Politicians, 1760–1770*. Manchester and New York: Manchester University Press.

Thomson, James (1981), *The Seasons*. J. Sambrook (ed.). Oxford: Clarendon Press.

Winchilsea, Anne (1974), *The Poems of Anne, Countess of Winchilsea*. M. Reynolds (ed.). New York: AMS Press.

Womersley, David (ed.) (1997), *Augustan Critical Writing*. London: Penguin Books.

Wordsworth, William (1988), *Lyrical Ballads: The text of 1798 edition with the additional 1800 poems and the Preface / Wordsworth and Coleridge*. R. L. Brett and A. R. Jones (eds). London and New York: Routledge.

Index